Rehearse Before You Retire

Third Edition Revised

also by ELMER OTTE

RETIREMENT REHEARSAL GUIDEBOOK

WELCOME RETIREMENT

Rehearse before you retire

by ELMER OTTE

*Third
Edition
Revised*

published by
RETIREMENT RESEARCH
P.O. BOX 401 • APPLETON, WISCONSIN 54911

Copyright © 1970, 1971, 1972, 1977 by Elmer A. Otte

Printed in the United States of America

Library of Congress Catalog Card Number 77-79286

Third Edition Revised

All rights reserved, no part of this book may be reproduced in any form or by any mechanical or electronic means without permission in writing from the publisher, except by a reviewer who may quote brief passages in a review.

Contents

A Personal Word 7
A Registered Letter—For You! 9
Preface 12

1. Begin by Rehearsing for Your Retirement . . 16
   - *Rehearsal Premise No. 1; 2; 3.*
   - *Action ideas to think about. A Quiz.*

2. Prepare To Retire *to* Something 55
   - *Time and Time Again—Activity.*
   - *Action ideas to think about. A Guide.*

3. Establish Sensible Retirement Expectations . 89
   - *Are You Ready to Slay These Dragons?*
   - *Action ideas to think about. A Response.*

4. Inventory Your Retirement Resources 117
   - *How Long Will You Need Retirement Income?*
   - *Action ideas to think about. An Income.*

5. Set Your Own Retirement Timetable 156
   - *When Will Retirement Happen to You?*
   - *Action ideas to think about. A List.*

6. Expect To Enjoy Your Retirement 182
   - *Career Women—and Singles.*
   - *Action ideas to think about. A Map.*

   NOTES ON ADDED SOURCES: 207
   - *Books*
   - *Organizations*

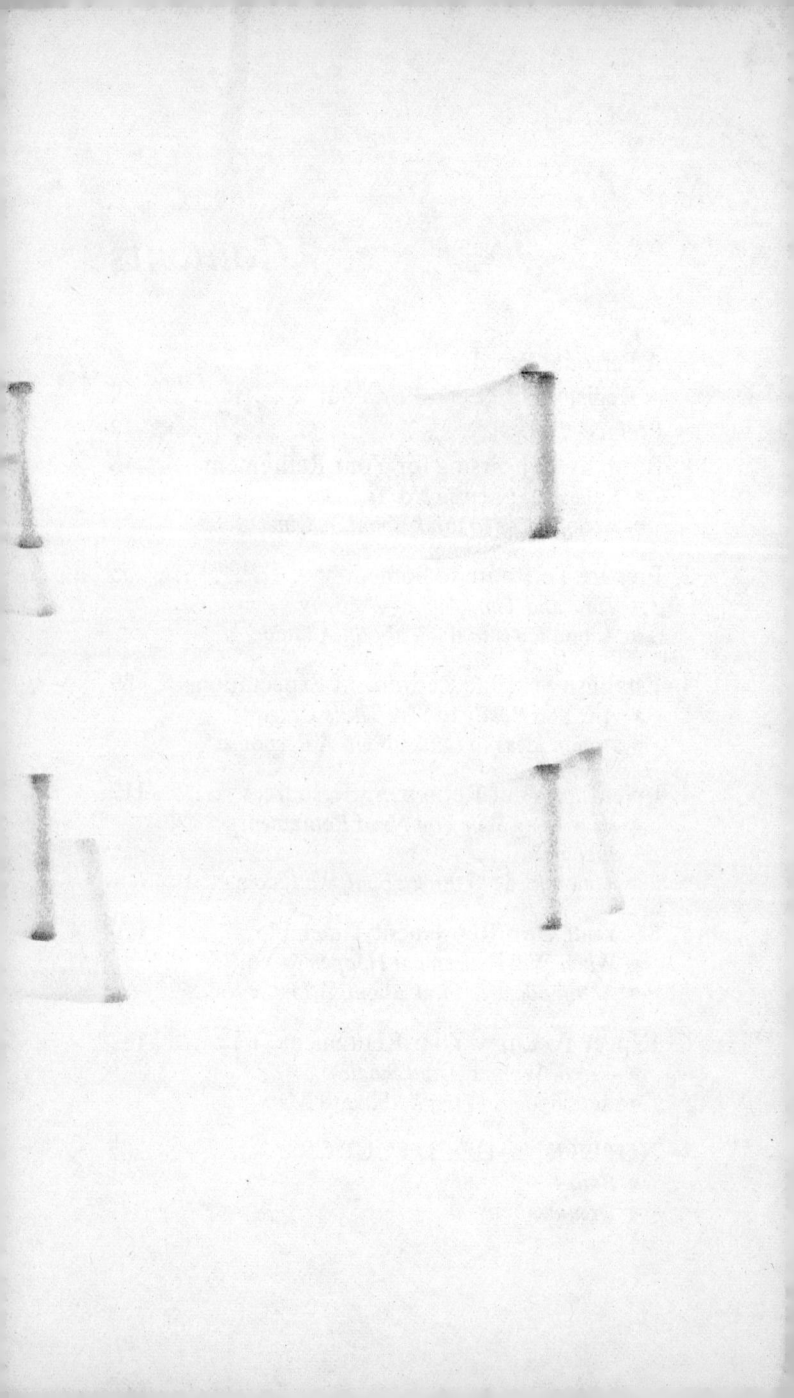

A Personal Word...

WHO ever heard of rehearsing for being out of a job? Out of almost everything except time?

We hear it often in the retirement fears and in the reported failures of too many retiring families. Successful retirees insist that some practice will indeed help make it "more" perfect.

For more than a decade I studied everything written on this subject. Books aplenty and an abundance of articles tell where to live pleasantly and inexpensively. Whether *he* should help around the house. Who should start small businesses—to keep busy and to pick up extra money. "Be sure to check in with social security" and so on ad relaxium. The information seems helpful enough.

But as I scouted around, peeking behind the problem from every angle, I concluded that it was often too late to learn about retirement—after retiring. One doesn't usually take piano lessons while giving a concert.

We decided together, as a family, how I could get readier—better and earlier—to make more sure that we would truly enjoy that promised land. That Utopian playground where life is all shaded by palm trees; where the friendly folks next door have no larger concern than where to park their golf cart; "and do you suppose our pension check will get here before we go off on holiday"—on holiday from all those other days of endless holidays?

What I discovered could fill a fat filing department—and it actually did.

Park bench interviews and curbstone surveys around the country proved that the problem is universal. Before-the-fact experts think they have the best solutions. One sector suggests that retiring early is the best goal. "As soon as we get a few more details straightened out." Another faction is alarmed that the day may come before they are ready.

A self-possessed and plan-ahead few anticipate it with calm joy.

Probably the only real secret our search turned up for sharing with you is that this hunt for answers just unearthed more questions—questions we will be examining happily and purposefully in these pages. We hope you enjoy the journey with us.

Elmer Otte
1977

A Registered Letter— For You!

```
REGISTERED
                    Mr. Walter Berkens
                    1125 Chappaqua Ave.,
                    Kokomo, Indiana 46901
```

Pause and reflect a moment on this thing which will surely happen one day to most of us. How much will it affect and change our working lifetime—and our retirement?

YOU have just received a registered letter. It's addressed to you and marked *personal and confidential*. What's in it?

Now try keeping it from each other. You open it.

10 REHEARSE BEFORE YOU RETIRE

- A message from your company president. The firm has been bought, sold or merged. New owners, new decisions, new problems—and new uncertainties.

- A message from your doctor. A report he is passing on about those medical tests you took at that clinic. They need to do more testing, to check further.

- A message from your best friend's widow. About Fred and how he had been warned to take it easy, and didn't. She's passing on these same over-work and over-worry warnings.

- A message from your son. His company finally gave him his big move. Now he can really do it big—and you, Dad and Mom, can relax a little. Maybe phase out earlier if you want.

- A message from your department head. He's sending it from the company's home office where he had been summoned. Serious budget cut-backs, functions dropped and people pruned.

One way or another people being pruned off of their lifetime tree of work—too often without adequate warning. Too often for too many men and their wives.

REHEARSE BEFORE YOU RETIRE

- It might be a message from personnel or pension people in your firm inviting you in to make a choice from several retirement options for your future.

How would you receive your own registered letter communique?

Panicked or peacefully prepared? It makes better sense to face the facts about retirement before they are facing you with their unfamiliar and unexpected details and conditions.

REHEARSE BEFORE YOU RETIRE is about getting ready—beforehand.

Preface

Too many men are afraid of the idea of retirement. Too bad. They should change their thinking—and plan to retire *to* something instead of retiring *from*.

Retirement ought to be a joyous goal—an idea worth dreaming about, a time we look forward to. Thinking about retiring can lighten the day's burden without distracting us too seriously from our duties.

A man may fear the boredom retirement might bring. Yet he very likely does little to prepare in advance—fixing to replace potential boredom with anticipation, with planning fun and excitement. He may suspect that he will miss his associates and friends yet he neglects to develop new contacts, new interests and new curiosities.

Most of us could use new friends, and new interests. People with perspective, fresh ideas and

REHEARSE BEFORE YOU RETIRE

new and far horizons. People who might teach us new habits or add lustre to tiresome old practices.

We lose our childlike sense of wonder and whimsy.

Many men are afraid they won't have enough money for retirement. Enough money for what? To live exactly as they and the Missus live now? Probably not. But it might be enough for a pleasant and happy retirement.

Most of the men still grimly shackled to their grindstones will be surprised to find that they will probably have as much money as they will need. As much as they will have time, appetite and energy for spending.

Besides, what's wrong with earning a little new money—in some new way?

Too many wives hide from too many foolish fears about their idea of retirement. One week they worry that the old boy won't last until retirement. Next time they are aghast at the thought of having him underfoot every day—all day—for evermore.

Many of these good women are right on both counts.

He may not make it. And if he does, they may have a difficult time getting adjusted to the idea of all that togetherness.

Wives should start worrying intelligently. On both parts of the problem. Their first reward may be a better chance for the husband to arrive at what can be a really fun time of life. And when he gets there, they may have the pleasant satisfaction of actually enjoying retirement—together.

If both members of a maturing marriage postpone their worrying, or if they plod along unthinkingly—without a plan—they will both have proved their fears well-founded, but for the wrong reasons.

If more couples would play make believe about how retirement could really be for them, more of them would get to enjoy it better. If more of them would *rehearse before they retire,* retirement might actually become a wonderful new time of life—for more people.

Most men work hard for forty years or more—no matter how much they protest to have enjoyed every minute of it.

Most wives worry hard for about the same number of years—no matter how much they actually enjoyed it.

Both deserve a chance at the happy change which their new life in retirement offers. Both have postponed often enough the fun and absence of pressure which such change promises—if they get ready.

There are too many widows.

They are said to own 85 per cent of the country's wealth. And yet, they do not seem to be enjoying their half of this fun and fortune—all by themselves. What went wrong?

How can more married partners avoid making the wrong turn? Or taking no turn at all? How

REHEARSE BEFORE YOU RETIRE

can more men side-step the ignominy of missing their own retirement? And how can more women make sure they will preserve their retirement partner?

If anticipation is half the joy of realization, then to *rehearse before you retire* should switch your attention from tension to pension.

If you and your bride have the maturity—and the imagination—to *rehearse before you retire,* you're the type whose retirement is bound to be fun.

If you are the driving—or the driven—type who must grind relentlessly on, to pause only to die ... with your boots on, blessings on you.

The world needs the dedicated and the resolute in order for a few of us blithe spirits to indulge ourselves—to provide the luxury of a loosened life line.

Better shop tomorrow for your own gold watch. Wind it smartly and set it for an early hour. Who said retirement meant lethargy? You've got plans to make and fetters to break. And then, you're due at your first rehearsal.

1

Begin by Rehearsing for Your Retirement

MOST people feel more secure if they get a guarantee with the products they buy. Guarantees promise satisfaction. Guarantees are comforting. They help us decide on particular products, on companies and their services.

It's time to tell you how you can get a 99.44 per cent gold-plated guarantee that your retirement will be a satisfactory one.

Comforted by this promise of guaranteed satisfaction, you might find yourself listening more intently to the details of how to bring it about—how to make sure your guarantee is merited, that it will be delivered to you with satisfaction.

Rehearsing for your retirement will help you find an abundance of pro and con answers, of plus and minus values, of do's and don't's—answers you

026 *Rehearsal Premise No. 1.*
  YOU ARE GOING TO BE RETIRED...
    a. *When you decide to retire; or—*
    b. *When "they" decide to retire you.*

Rehearsal Premise No. 2.
  KEEP CONTROL OF "WHEN"—PREPARE BEFOREHAND...
    a. *Stay involved in your own security;*
    b. *Make ready your own alternatives.*

Rehearsal Premise No. 3
  RETIREES WHO DO PREPARE DO ENJOY IT MORE...
    a. *Abundant evidence proves this fact;*
    b. *They create a pleasant expectation;*
    c. *And, enjoy a busy, happy, longer life.*

have personally experienced. It will demonstrate how retirement in one circumstance would be undesirable for you, while in another you and your spouse could find happy satisfaction for the rest of your restful years.

Much of the world's progress is the result of planned and meaningful rehearsal. Show business and its talented people spend more time in rehearsals than they do in putting on performances. That's why the performances please critical reviewers and today's sophisticated audiences.

Even boy-girl romancing has historically been, and is still considered in some quarters to be, a rehearsal for more foolproof marriages.

Golfers are admonished to practice to perfect their games. Industry trains its workers to improve their skills and performance. Even geniuses rehearse their specialties toward their own goals of perfection.

Why not rehearse for your retirement?

WHAT'S to rehearse to retire, you ask? Let's take a look at the first day after you have been patted on the head by your superiors, slapped on the back by your peers and sent into that fearsome wonderland of retirement.

You both sleep late—or try to. Finally after a good deal of tossing and thinking, you get up—pretty much as you always have. Perhaps, tomorrow you will sleep a little later—after you get used to the idea of not answering to anyone any more.

REHEARSE BEFORE YOU RETIRE

You wander around the house picking up magazines, running your finger over some of the books on your shelves. (Must read some of these now that I'll have all this time.) You stare out of the window, dreamily imagining all of the delicious days you'll have with nothing to do. Breakfast never smelled better. You sigh contentedly as you join your wife at the table.

"Happy?"

"Guess so!"

"Well—what do you want to do today?"

"Don't know yet."

"Remember now—you can do anything you want."

"That's right, anything. But probably not everything."

You'll read a book maybe. Or go fishing. Or walk in the park or the woods. Take a ride somewhere. Fool around in your workroom. Go to the library. Always wanted to take the time to really do the museum. Go shopping with the Missus. Fix that sticky back door.

What about tomorrow? And the next day?

Travel? Trip around the world would be nice. Good for both of you. Give you time to decide what you want to do. What about when you get back—if you go? Move out West maybe. Or try the South. Move somewhere. What's wrong with right here?

A man may retire from the rat race, but he

doesn't resign from the human race. Neither does his wife.

Better if they have planned for this strange new time—planned it in some detail—and rehearsed those plans to see whether they will work. To see whether those rehearsals can help them put together a really good show. Better if they are retiring *to* something. Something they have practiced for so that they are reasonably sure they are going to enjoy it. Every blessed, new, delightful, long retirement day of it.

What's to rehearse?

Practice running through those day-after-day routines to satisfy yourselves that you won't flip your lid if that's all you have to do. Find out beforehand if you will need more than all that nothing to fill each day after day. To try cottage living or apartment living. Playing golf every day all week if that is your bent. Or to play bridge with people you meet on your rehearsal vacations. Tour the countryside; visit the beaches and boating marinas if this appeals.

Better fiddle around with your uncertainties and your little dreams while you are still employed, while you can take three or four-week vacations to experiment. To make mistakes you won't have to live with. To get those silly ideas out of your system. Or—to satisfy yourself that this is indeed what you want to do. What both of you want to do. There is comfort in knowing where you're going, what you'll be doing, whether you'll be enjoying it.

REHEARSE BEFORE YOU RETIRE 21

THERE is a lot to rehearse to help you retire more successfully.

Satisfaction can be guaranteed—but you're the one who will write your own warranty, put your own stamp, your own acceptance on it.

It's refreshing to see how others have rehearsed for their retirement and how they're making out.

Take Sam, a very successful industrial salesman. A couple of minor heart spasms scared a few years off his wife and threatened to shorten his life. He decided to look around to find what he would like to do so that he might retire a little early. To save himself so that they could still enjoy themselves, despite his coronary concerns.

Sam learned how to tune pianos.

I guess it's possible to take lessons to learn how to do almost anything. I hear you can still go to school to learn to shoe horses. That is certainly a passing craft even though riding stables, riding and racing horses still abound. Who sees that they stay shod?

But Sam learned all about tuning pianos. Then one day he resigned from his sales territory and moved to a modest and charming little community in one of the southeastern states.

I can hear all those questions now: "Sam's a newcomer in a town that's new to him in a southern circumstance where a "damn Yankee salesman" may have to have a little extra good luck in his human relationships in order to permanently enjoy it. In order to be accepted and become one with the community." Sam was a salesman, remember? He knows how to relate to people anywhere. He knew how to *do something*. And he found out that the people in his new home town needed the services of a piano tuner.

He found that out before he moved there. He rehearsed the entire proposition on a vacation or two in order to make sure that he wouldn't be trying to "shoe horses if oxen were still pulling the plows."

Sam set himself up in the piano tuning business by inserting a notice in the local paper. He ran a few small announcement ads telling of his hope to serve all of his new neighbors who had pianos which were undoubtedly long since out of tune. He set up a schedule of tuning one piano each forenoon. That gave him a half day off every day.

Sam got acquainted around the community. He made friends because he was a friendly fellow. He made some new money because he was a good piano tuner. He and his wife began making a good life in retirement because he had retired *to* something and they had rehearsed to guarantee success.

It almost spoils Sam's story to add that he has by now become just a little busier at tuning a few more pianos than he had had in mind. But he says he can control this growing demand as well as his ambition to serve his new "out-of-tune" neighbors. Sam

REHEARSE BEFORE YOU RETIRE 23

remembers that for some years no one had been tuning their pianos.

A number of his tuning commitments came from the local school system. The principal was a fellow service club member. He suggested Sam come over and take a look at the pianos—all ten of them—in the various schools in their town. Sam appraised each of the neglected instruments, set a suggested schedule for putting them in tune, added a schedule for periodic maintenance and added his annual fee for the service.

The kids in Sam's newly adopted retirement community probably still stick books behind the felt piano hammers to upset assembly and recital performers but the school board and the community are becoming aware that the equipment is now in good hands, Sam's good hands.

How is his health? Sam paces himself. He is happy at doing something new. He's not driven by old ambitions, never ending quotas and hard-driving sales supervisors.

Sam and the Missus enjoy long "vacation" weekends and take longer jaunts whenever they hanker to go north or west—or wherever. Since Sam can schedule his piano tuning appointments according to his own needs, he's in charge of his new life. Sam says it works because he tried it out before he made his move. Sam insists that the limited time and little money he invested in learning this happy new skill for his retirement years was one of the wiser investments he ever made. One that pays him bigger dividends than many of his old stock market wheeling and dealing days. Sam and his wife have a good life. Now he's learning to improve his piano playing ability as well.

I know another man who worked in a paper mill. He had a couple of extracurricular jobs. His mill job had to do with shipping department functions which didn't satisfy all of his energies since lift trucks lightened his work. Neither did his paycheck satisfy all of his needs to help put his kids through college. This man was a beekeeper on the side. He kept between 100 and 200 hives of bees. Bees take an exacting amount of work and care to keep them healthy, fed and happy.

During the blossom seasons, our mill-hand beekeeper had to spend a fair number of after hours adding compartments onto the hives to provide the bees with sufficient room—for filling the hives with honey.

I was once staggered to learn that in good years his bee hives had produced as much as 12 tons of honey. To say nothing of all of the beeswax he sold to pharmaceutical wholesalers and honey houses.

What in the world would anyone do with 12 tons of honey?

This beekeeper sells honey regionally in consumer-sized pails and jars, and even in old-fashioned honeycombs. The rest is marketed in 60-pound cans

REHEARSE BEFORE YOU RETIRE 25

to bakers or through honey wholesalers across the country.

When our beekeeper friend retired from his job in the mill, he concentrated on bees and honey. I asked, after the beginning of his first new season in retirement, which he began at 60, how many hives or swarms he had purchased for this first full time "retirement" season. He said 150—about the same as always. He reminded me that he had retired and that he saw no reason to increase one job after having decreased the other.

Where to live in retirement can be a considerable problem to a lot of us. We yearn for a cool climate in the summer and warmer breezes with less snow and ice when its colder. When we retire we think we might go south in the winter, coming north in the summer. This takes more than just money. It takes a total relocation ability which is not practical to many of us. Friends of ours named Carroll did it wonderfully well. They bought one of those travel trailers and had it accommodated to their automobile. When they retired from their retail establishment, they took off for Texas and spent a number of months looking around, attending concerts and plays, visiting museums—and playing golf. Then they wandered around the Gulf Coast east into Florida and eventually up into the Carolinas to which they had also been attracted.

They wrote glowingly about a particular place in one of the Carolinas which had a combination of seaside, Southern charm—and golf courses. They told about their neighbors at the trailer park sites where they lived and where they visited. They reported about their improving golf game. Later they wandered westward and worked their way up the Pacific Coast into Oregon and Washington because these areas had also interested them over the years.

Finally we heard from them from one of the valleys of California. It seemed they might be thinking of settling into a retirement community which was developing there. No comment about golf this time. Ultimately, they did settle in an Arizona retirement community in the vicinity of Phoenix where their cottage, which now replaced their travel trailer, opened onto not one but two golf courses.

Now besides spending half days listening to their record collection in a manner for which their studies had prepared them, they played golf—daily or oftener.

She still lives there. She had written us from many of the far corners she has visited around the world—to tell us of golf scores and of her visits to these interesting places—activities which she is continuing —as a widow.

DIFFERING points of view have been expressed about whether senior citizens might enjoy—or should even consider—living in retirement communities. Especially referred to here are those retirement complexes which include recreation buildings

REHEARSE BEFORE YOU RETIRE

with arts and crafts, and other hobby facilities, church and social centers and the like. The question of whether these are helpful or a good idea is probably a personal one. Some people like the continual involvement with friends of like circumstances and like interests. Some do not.

Senior Cities have been derisively called used car lots for people, hardly a guaranteed haven of happiness for those who must now live away from families and friends. Each extreme view probably fits some people but it does work well for many.

The point to be made here is that each interested prospect for any kind of retirement living ought to take out the almost no-cost insurance of spending some time visiting a selection of such centers—to try to rehearse and to establish as well as possible whether or not he or she, or they, would enjoy this kind of living. If it appeals, it can be very nice indeed with much of the aloneness wiped out by a lot of togetherness. If the idea appalls, those who are more personally resourceful will quickly know from testing it. Each can then be more assured with his personal decision to "join in the fun"—or to "go it alone."

One of the best ways to plan a trip is to begin by making a list of places you want to visit. This establishes distances, times needed for travel, costs involved in getting there and back. It establishes preferences, ruling out some of the less favorite and gives you a budgeting and timetable basis which is realistic.

Most of us who have taken auto trips have contacted some of the major oil companies or the automobile clubs for their help in planning routes to take, places to visit, things to see and problems and opportunities to expect. I think these things are sometimes called tour guides. The idea is to develop your own road map or to secure one to help you decide where you are going, what it takes to get there and the time and money involved.

It might be a good idea to take a map of the United States and to divide it into four sections by drawing a line from north to south approximately at the Mississippi River and a line from east to west at approximately the Mason-Dixon line. This segmenting of the country into four sections begins the process of isolating in a broad way where one might wish to investigate retirement living. One can go still further by dividing these quarters into further quarters—or by segmenting the map more definitively so that special retirement appeal areas can be set apart from each other, to establish preference priorities.

Deciding which part of the country one might wish to investigate has to do with what appeals. Is it a warmer climate, a drier one, a cooler one, a lazier one or one with a more vigorous atmosphere? It pays to set down preferences and to pursue them until we find we didn't really like that idea

REHEARSE BEFORE YOU RETIRE 29

anyway. Often people are attracted to regions they know about from the experience of friends or families, or from having visited there.

The reasons for picking places are not important. Methods of taking out some of the guesswork are available to all. Making maps, plans and charts of places to go and things to do are a first step. From these investigations one can begin the process of writing for the literature of these places. It would be surprising to most people to see how much high quality informational help is available from just about any place your heart desires to examine.

Draw your blueprint carefully as you dream lazily before a winter's fire or laze in a swinging summer hammock. Imagine how it will be when you are retired there.

Folks we have known have segmented the country in just this way and made their own chart of retirement goals. These have been checked out over the period of the several years preceding their actual retirement through the use of vacation trips to targeted areas. Most of us have frittered away vacation days in places selected to please one partner or to bore the other—or to accommodate the wishes of families or friends.

Lots of families have taken a few long-trip vacations with their children. How did these work out? Were there favored places you responded to as you stopped here and there on your journeys? What about using the next couple of vacation periods for going to such preferred places for the purpose of further checking them out?

Try to put a little fun into this rehearsal business. You are learning how to live after you have finished working. Decide what you want to learn from the experience. Plan your visits and each day's activities sensibly in advance but without the straightjacket regimen of normal work schedules. Drive or fly there or take a cross-country bus for the purpose of getting next to a lot of people to find out what their views are about places and things to do and see. Find out if your own trip rehearsal works for you. You will enjoy the experience for its own sake and probably will eliminate many places. Isn't that better than having waited until retirement time to reach these decisions? Pick and choose from among those places which remain most attractive?

REHEARSING for retirement has to do with many things. It has to do with how we will spend our days. It has to do with determining how far dollars will go. It can tell us something about what we are going to do day-after-day, year-after-year. It gives us a chance to experiment with turning hobbies and other burning interests into avocational or full-time activities. It can tell us where we want to be geographically, climatically, economically and according to many other criteria.

It has been most amazing in this study of

Dispatch Phone Number 624-5411

REHEARSE BEFORE YOU RETIRE

planning for retirement to find how well so many are doing the job all by themselves in their own way.

One that stands out as an exciting example is the man and wife team who studied mushrooms. They were admittedly not wealthy and yet they had traveled many places in their own hemisphere and had also taken a number of trips to the European continent in search of added mushroom lore. He was becoming an in-depth authority on the varieties of mushrooms available in these regions. He also became a considerable expert in close-up color photography of mushrooms. As he found new mushrooms in new places, he captured slides upon slides of what he had found. These were all carefully catalogued according to his planned pattern because he was building a lecture presentation—a portfolio made up of the joys of his journeys, of the slides of their mushroom experience from the world's woods and fields which they had visited. He had accumulated a vast store of interesting data about where mushrooms are found and why, about those which are food and those which are to be feared. Our friend became, as a result of his consuming interest and hobby, one of our leading experts on mushrooms without having been formally trained or having been taken by the hand by anyone. Just his own interests and ambitions.

His after-work world promises to be full of fascinating contacts with people with the same kind of interests, with people from all walks of business or professional life who have also found in the mushroom a world of fascination and excitement.

Some dollars will surely come back to him now as he speaks and shows his slides to clubs and at museums, but the pleasure he brings won't begin to match his own satisfaction which he will receive from the bringing.

Mushrooms seem to lead people into all kinds of new directions. We know another mushroom devotee who also had an interest in stained glass work. He has now combined the two so that he is a qualified teacher and lecturer on mushrooms, their life and times—and on how to make stained glass windows and artifacts. His subjects have often included the muted colors of the mushrooms he has loved and learned so much about.

His stained glass hangings of nodding morels must be seen to be appreciated. They are just another dimension of the minds, appetites and attitudes which reach out for the joy and fun of living which has prepared most of us in some special way so that we dare presume to specialize. To pursue even more purposefully anything we want, any place we want, almost any time.

The use of vacation days for the pursuit of hobbies pays off. There is a renewal in the re-creation that comes from activity and from the excitement of mounting enthusiasms for things that are not dreary and daily humdrum. What would you like to do? What would you like to become skilled at

REHEARSE BEFORE YOU RETIRE

doing? Such learning is available most places. Or it can be pursued in vacation days by going wherever the knowledge exists.

Increasingly shorter hours each week and our expanding leisure time offer segments of the clock and the calendar for all who will plan to grasp this opportunity and these new purposes for themselves.

Leisure to rehearse new things, to try new places, to meet new people. Will it be squandered and lost? Or will it be conserved and husbanded toward pre-determined goals? This probably depends on how we dream and how we harness those dreams to help us earn maximum retirement realities.

Our own retirement research, planning and rehearsal philosophies—as just one example—are the direct result of more than ten years of examining the entire retirement subject.

We began simply to serve ourselves and our family. As time went on the subject and scope expanded in interest and involvement. We gathered files and rooms full of data, exhibits, information and helpful hints about where to retire and how to retire better. When to get started in order to avoid pitfalls others had discovered.

One inevitably becomes expert on any subject that gets one's principal attention in a concentrated way over a long period of time. We became expert on retirement data and were admonished by friends and colleagues to share this knowledge through lectures, articles, pamphlets—in book form and in training seminars for industry and its organizations.

Our own preparation began with reading. This led us into in depth research in libraries and at vacation meccas. I started to talk on the subject among my friends and with their friends. I wrote on the subject. Some of what I wrote was published. I was encouraged to keep writing because of the vast store of data that grew and grew. Cataloguing, clipping, filing and rereading filled my pores with facts, figures and fancies about the wonderful world of retirement for many people—and also about the staggering struggle to improve retirement quality by beginning to plan earlier. Planning more intelligently and rehearsing where, how and when.

Probably the best possible way to get rid of the delusion of full time fishing, of years of daily golf or of sitting at the seashore for the rest of your life is to go there now and try it just that way. If you're still a bug on any of these ideas when you have finished filling your pores and stuffing yourself with the satisfaction of it all, why not think seriously about building exactly this kind of retirement life around what you like most?

If you find that either you or your spouse lose interest or find your appetites too easily satisfied, too quickly sated from all this change, then retirement may not be the time for you to fool around full-time this way. Find something else—or a

REHEARSE BEFORE YOU RETIRE

combination of other ideas and places. Most of our lives are made up of numbers of activities and interests. Why not expect that retirement will be somewhat like the rest of our lives? Except that we will have more time to do as we please, to enjoy our best enthusiasms.

Friends have told us that the idea of rehearsing for retirement certainly works in practice. They have gone off for weeks on end pursuing some exciting fascination, only to find that they have quickly burned up early fervor, to become bored with dullness. They were just about as excited at having learned this in advance as they might have been had it worked better for them. Most people report that their long time and sincere interests transfer well into retirement and that the pursuit of them is just dandy. They just need to fill out their available energies and days with still a few additional and compatible interests and pursuits. Some fortunate ones have found the scope of their fascinations to be so much more broad than they had imagined. They simply will never in their remaining lifetimes have enough time to sample all their particular situation offers or to fulfill all of the awakened ambitions they have found in their chosen objectives.

Each to his own. But each to something, to some place and to some purpose. Each better prepared and better assured that it will work in reality because it has been practiced and rehearsed for in happy pretending.

Since preparation for retirement *to* something is an awareness thing, a pleasant preoccupation for some of us more wayward workers, it is apt to happen to us, to come into our minds any time after age 40—but more typically after age 50. By then our backs are bent a bit by our burdens. We are getting filled to overflowing with the futilities and the frustrations of not enjoying as much progress as we had dreamed of making.

We see what others are getting done. We are reminded by our spouses to take it easier, by our doctor to take it easier—and by our bosses to take it less easy. We begin thinking about quitting—at some distant time in the future, of course. Like tomorrow. Or next month or next year. We are not permitted to linger long in such irresponsible reverie. Our practical world jolts us back into hard reality.

However, it is probably not transgressing too seriously for those who do apply their best energies to their principal purpose in life if they also begin the process of enjoying some scheming and dreaming. Anticipating the life and times when they won't be driven so madly down through the rigors of their particular rut into oblivion. Escape periodically into thinking about how it will be when you can spend lots more time just being all by yourselves, without the pressures of your particular rat race.

These retirement reveries are not jobs that get done well in just a year or two. If that's all the time you have left it still figures that you ought to

REHEARSE BEFORE YOU RETIRE

make the most of it for shaking some of the bugs out of your unsolved scheduling, out of your uncharted timetable. It's time to look a little further ahead.

Like establishing a five-year plan for trying more things, for settling on where to go, what to do, how to live and all that. For practicing which of all our areas of fascination we really prefer to retire *to*.

In setting down your own plan, set up alternate timetables. Make it age 65, or 62, or five years from now—or however works out according to the criteria which have a bearing on which time goal will be best for you.

When we wrote to the chambers of commerce in all of the preferred areas of the United States in which we might be pleased to retire, we were staggered by the amount of data available.

We were astounded at the friendly, personal interest and the involvement of those responsible to attract new people to particular communities or areas. We have been personally invited to stop in, to get acquainted, to have questions answered. All of this seems to have resulted from the fact that we began setting down a five-year and a ten-year plan and have therefore spent time establishing our own road map to tell us where we want to go and how we plan to get there.

If this planning fixation keeps being repeated a few times too often it is because it can't be said too many times to make it important to many more people and to a greater degree than appears presently to be general practice.

We have a doctor friend in Iowa who told this story. He had long been a camera nut, active in local camera clubs. He was especially active in his dark room, developing, enlarging, dodging, finishing, testing and experimenting with mat papers, glossy papers and the like to enhance his artistry and probably to help justify expensive and extensive camera equipment. I suppose it follows that after so many thousands of dollars and so many uncounted hours, one must have taken most of the close-ups of most of the pussy willows in one's county. One has shot all of the pigtails of all of the little girls in the neighborhood and all of the freckled-faced boys who roam our area. Close-up portraits and candid views of most of the relatives who permit such indulgence. By now one has been rebuffed repeatedly by bored protestations when these filmed delights have been shown—with all of the shades drawn, of course.

As this doctor got close to his own retirement, he found a ready-made solution which combined the best of both of his worlds. He liked people and wanted to continue to be involved with them. He knew a whale of a lot about cameras and their capabilities. He got a part-time job in a large shopping center in his community where he quickly became the new camera expert. Appointments can be made or he may be found at his counter—with all his

REHEARSE BEFORE YOU RETIRE 39

enthusiasms showing—on any Friday or Saturday, or as otherwise advertised.

Imagine his satisfactions at being able to share all he had learned, all that he had experienced and studied. To do it for real take home pay, on a part-time basis. His new job keeps him out of the house and out of his dark room. It keeps a little money coming in and a lot of expertise going out, to be used by people who don't know one end of a shutter from an overexposure.

This type of example is not unlike hundreds of other experiences you and I have had which we can polish up and sell at our own time and pace. The going rate is just fine if we bring a real service to meet a real need. It puts continued involvement into our daily lives. We don't have to do it down the street if we would rather live in Florida, or Arizona or Vermont. We can find a duplication almost anywhere of all of the facilities and economic structures that will accommodate just about anything we know that's worth sharing. Be it guns and their trajectory, or cameras and their magic. Or it might be TV and its mysteries, or shoes with their fit and fashion foibles. What have you done, working your way through school, in hobbies or in work that can be translated into a scaled down avocational occupation? Now that you desire to drift slowly into less pressured pastures, avoid becoming preoccupied full time.

If you are professionally expert as an accountant, as a lawyer or as a bank trust authority, you have something very important to sell. It's needed by others who are already retired or by those hovering uncertainly on the threshold with their house not quite in order. The business includes having one's estate neatly planned, fixed up for the family and not for the tax people. No restrictions regarding high or low economic levels. Everybody has some economic worth now that we are still all living and benefiting from socialized security.

Visit any senior center in your area. Sit and talk with the people who are living those lives now. Visit particularly with those who are older. You will discover dozens of different ways for you and your spouse to find new satisfaction and enjoyment in bringing comfort, help and advice to such people who may really need it. Perhaps this is where you will find your niche in retirement. It is also a thing that needs doing right now—for its own sake.

Even the exciting and exhilarating panics and crises of the advertising business finally get to those who labor no matter how lovingly as potential lunatics in that harried asylum. Each must find his own way to jump his own ship. As soon as one can get his house a little more in order. As soon as "they" drive us to it—whether we are ready or not.

Some quit to write books that sell poorly. Some sell their creative skills free lance. Most yearn for quiet retreats in exotic climes where the world can't get at them any more. Others wander off into

REHEARSE BEFORE YOU RETIRE 41

island waters, to fall in love with the lazy way they find there. You find them visiting real estate offices, checking with local citizenry about a little cottage on a high hill. No matter how much it will take to bring it out of the shack category. No matter how charming. A number of my promotional friends are already in the process of building something a notch above peasant accommodations on such islands. A lot of hard working, talented people are preparing for new lives in these new circumstances. It isn't important that anyone other than those who are digging around to solve their particular retirement dreaming be pleased.

It's a good idea when you wander off on rehearsal reconnoitering to carry extra walking-around money. It helps to find out whether your appetite has too high a price tag. Often we have found it possible to combine less luxurious programs with slightly more practical daily routines, to bring in a few inflated dollars even with deflated purchasing power. It helps level off high prices, to match them with our lower incomes. Whether you work or not depends on your personal preference and on your circumstances. Perhaps you are the kind who would be too bored to rack it all up and never lift another finger.

There is certainly no end to the needs of people out there—needs which must be satisfied by others than themselves. Perhaps you don't need new money but rather need the time and the freedom to share generously from your store of talent—to help solve some of the unsolved problems which haunt others of the human race who are not as fortunate as we.

Face it. Not everyone has strong hobby skills. What we have been doing in our daily work may not be something the world can quickly accommodate. Some skills take $500,000 worth of plant machinery to make them useful. You may have run a punch press, a pants press or an electronic computer. Or you may have served your county as agricultural supervisor for farm and urban citizens. Stop to think how many of your countrymen do not have these special skills or this special knowledge. Most of us know how to do many things that need doing in underprivileged areas. These underprivileged places and people are just about everywhere—down our own block among boys and girls whose fathers are too busy making their pile or whose mothers are not sufficiently interested to find what it is the kids would enjoy doing which will turn them into mature and responsible citizens when their turn comes.

If you do not know where to go to rehearse for your particular brand of retirement living, why not get in touch with the multitude of agencies which struggle with needs that are not being met. Have you thought of contacting Vista, the Peace Corps, Job Corps, Head Start Programs or the United Nations to find out elementary things which anyone can help with?

REHEARSE BEFORE YOU RETIRE

There are governmental agency bulletins and hordes of governmental publications which are inexpensive to write for. By writing to Superintendent of Documents, U.S. Government Printing Office in Washington, D.C., one will find more things to do, more things that need doing and more things that each of us can relate to than you have days left in which to get it all done.

Want more rehearsal ideas?

Are you a genealogy buff? Lots of folks would like to know where Grandpa came from. To get their family tree trimmed with all the aunts and uncles neatly lined up, including those long hidden in closets. Try special libraries, like the Newberry in Chicago for historic reference and family tree data.

Have you ever thought of driving a school bus? It's a great way to stay close to kids, to bring safety and comfort to little people—and it needs doing everywhere.

If you were to go today to any community you thought you'd like to retire in, you could find grandparent and babysitting opportunities. If you can't stand kids any more, there's pet-sitting and pet-boarding for those who know how to handle hounds, kittens or baby alligators.

It's fun to answer ads in the newspapers one can subscribe to. Any city you have in mind. Subscribe for a month and read every local ad. Answer more than you are seriously interested in to see what you will find. There's need out there. All you have to do is get your name tag tied to it. There's need for help. There's opportunity for income, for satisfaction, for making the kind of contribution that will fill your retirement days.

It's no great trick to know how to begin if you prepare to retire *to* something. To begin the process of rehearsing for a retirement that you probably cannot thoroughly imagine all by yourself. You have to rehearse to find out what more you need to know so that you don't foul it up when you finally get settled there.

Let's take a trip.

Let's hop an airplane and fly either east or west—or north or south. Set down in any airport any place. Hop a local area bus and wander off into the most pleasant little town you find at the foot of the hill, on the bluff overlooking the sea or a river or on the rolling plains. It's important to have a view—a view that stretches out to new horizons. You are looking for a place you want to be. A place you want to live. To meet new people and new problems, to help solve some of them with the help of these new neighbors.

This is a different way to rehearse before you retire—different from looking over retirement communities and senior citizen center complexes.

Each place—each method—has its worth and each appeals to different kinds of people.

Go down to the Chamber of Commerce or

REHEARSE BEFORE YOU RETIRE

the information office maintained by the local advancement association. Stop in at City Hall or the County Court House. Get acquainted. Tell them you're thinking of coming to live in their town and you'd like to learn all about it. Not so much about who runs the place, who's important, who's in charge.

Rather what do people do here? What are they like? What are they interested in? What kinds of problems are there in the community that need someone to help with? Don't sound like an expert from out of town with all the answers. They'll know you're a warm and friendly human being if that's what you really are. They'll know that you can help them, help local folks enjoy life better, to have new hope, to dream new dreams—if that's how you sound, sincerely.

They'll probably be wary of quick and easy answers to the problems they have lived with for centuries. At least for generations. Problems they've gotten so used to they have probably forgotten they exist. Find the place and find the folks to whom you can relate, to whom both you and the Missus can relate. Find the place you'd like to be.

Go to the local library and read local history. Be careful to tell the librarian that's what you'd like to look into because you're thinking of coming there to live. Research her. She's apt to be a wise woman (or more and more—a bright young man) with intelligent and sensible insights into what these local neighbors would like to accomplish, what their unanswered prayers are.

Gather all of the literature about the region. Wander off into the hills, into neighboring towns, to the lakes, to the little restaurants where people gather for a social cup of coffee in mid-morning. Don't intrude but don't be reluctant to be drawn into neighborly conversation. See how they respond to your gestures. Measure how you respond to them. Do you think you could get used to this place, to like its people? Do you think there are "pianos to tune here, horses that need shoeing," kids who need adopted grandparents to sit with them? Older people who need someone to fix their hair, to read them stories, to write their letters? Do you bring something for these people? Will they accept you and what you have to offer, in gracious kindness and in warm regard?

If you still feel good about where you are and about these new neighbors you're looking over, and if they're still friendly and helpful after looking you over, you have probably found a pretty good place to begin rehearsing for your retirement.

If not, move on.

There are some towns that lack the personality certain individuals may be looking for. Let that be the town for others. Go where you're wanted, welcomed and needed, and dig in. Rehearse by "counting all the pianos" quietly. Number "the horses that need shoeing." Take a look at the local

REHEARSE BEFORE YOU RETIRE

paper and visit with its editor. He's probably harassed by all the job printing he promised to deliver last week and hasn't yet begun. But if it's a nice town he's probably a pretty good philosopher and a pretty good pipeline to how you'd like it here.

Stop in at the bank. Sit down and talk to the head man there. And don't be surprised if it's a woman. Or a very young man. It might be a branch bank. These people know what's going on. It's their money that helps turn the wheels of most of the local enterprises.

Join in watching those wheels turn to see how fortune spins here. Find out where the wheels squeak and think about how you might help oil them. Are you challenged to remain here, or are you restless to roar out of town? Take your cue from how you feel.

And if it should come to pass that you don't find any happy harbors in your looking around, over a period of time, after a number of careful studies and a number of good beginnings, maybe you aren't the kind that should wander off into the world's wilderness to make your new way. Not each of us is suited to every pathway that beckons. Find it out ahead of time and retreat without any threat of loss. Better to do it before than when your risk is greater later.

One of the things you ought to do if you find the place you think you'd like to live is set up a regular living program for a week or two. Rent a room in a hotel or motel—or even in a home where you can get closer to people. Do a walk-through of your future and figure out how you'd spend your time. All that time when you wouldn't be helping your new neighbors solve their old problems.

After all, you are going to be retired. You are going to be free. You are going to be taking it easy. Loafing and enjoying your earned leisure. You are going to try fishing in new waters. Hiking along new trails. Picking up seashells along new shores. Visiting with new friends. Eating in their familiar inns and listening to their old tales which will be new to you. How does it wear? How does your new role feel—in your new play? Do you think you will act your part well and do you think your world will enjoy the performance once the show is ready?

Women have a big stake in the retirement of their bread winner. Women ought to be about as interested as anyone in the rehearsal process. It's going to be important that they are happy with what they're going to be doing, where they're going to be doing it.

It's just as important as his reaction. You're both going to be spending your lives there. Chances are you might be spending a few more years than he in your new place unless you should decide—either in advance or later—that you would ultimately return to where home used to be. In any event, pay attention Madam. It's your retirement too. Everyone is weary of that trite old line about "less than half

REHEARSE BEFORE YOU RETIRE 49

the income and more than twice the husband" but you had both better face it because that's how it will be.

Of course, if you're one of those close family people who needs to have all your uncles and cousins close by, you won't even be off on any of these silly junkets looking for new harbors to dock in. That's up to you—to both of you. But if you came along in reasonably good spirit, give this try a chance because retirement ought to be the reward that it promises. If not, someone will have shortchanged you unnecessarily. Retirement is time off. Time off for good behavior. You've earned it. Why don't you both prepare to enjoy it?

THERE'S a lot of advice for wives whose husbands are tiptoeing toward the twilight time of retirement. Most pertains to what you do back home, *before* he retires. Things like getting your fiscal house in order. Agreeing to live with the kind of order you get it in. You probably aren't going to be the richest new arrivals on these new beaches anyway. You weren't back home. If you happen to be loaded, work out a program for letting it fly delightfully through your fingers. Or make your pile produce even more. Share some of it with those who really need it. Help some of those who need so much help. Or—just plain enjoy it together.

You ladies will certainly have helped wean the old boy away from work habits and job hobbies.

Better begin filling that vacuum, beforehand. That's why rehearsal junkets are such a good idea. Gives him the feeling that other worlds out there are waiting for him.

Wives need to form new partnerships with their husbands as they approach retirement. They'll probably be together more but the partnership will be different. It might be in a new place. It might have to squeak along on less money. Most do. But they manage. There are strange places, strange faces and new customs to get used to. Most women are good at making new friends. They can help their husbands in this. When you are helping plan for retirement don't treat it as his foolish idea. Make it yours, too. Recognize that it is inevitable to be a new life for both of you. There's little you can do to escape it. Might as well count on enjoying it.

Wives can help negligent husbands get their health house in order before they retire. If there's anything that can still be done about the shape he's in by then. Get him checked out just as you would get your car checked out. So that it won't be breaking down within the first five years. Do the same, but much more delicately, with regard to your joint relationship to your religion—if you are practicing one. Get all of your houses in order. Plan to enjoy the comforts of health, of peace and security.

When the time for retirement comes and you are ready to play your duet as you have rehearsed it, retiring *to* some place and *to* something, promise to

REHEARSE BEFORE YOU RETIRE 51

do one more helpful thing. Try to keep old George away from those artificial retirement parties. Unless that is awfully important to him.

Such affairs are full of empty words, so much emotional excitement. The only guy who gets really worked over is the fellow that it's all about. It doesn't seem to be as kind as it is intended to be. They may make a fellow feel they couldn't have managed without him but they had often reminded him they could have done so joyfully long ago. Views vary on retirement parties but I suggest that the two of you elope—before it happens. This one point is important. *Don't let him go back to the scene of his working crimes.* He has retired. Retirement means he doesn't work there any more. Others who are there are supposed to be working. They can't do anything but interrupt what they ought to be doing to tell him things he shouldn't be hearing.

It's a touch sad to see them come back, to hang around, to bother and to bore their old brothers. Worse yet to come back and to be ignored by those who are honestly busy and who can't understand those who aren't.

Finally, treat your mutual preparation for your mutual retirement *to* something—by holding a number of sensible rehearsals that are trying to accomplish something. Remember your purpose. Remember your goals. Take another look at your list of objectives for retirement. What do you think you really want to do in your retirement years?

Experiment. Test. Try this and try that. Reject what bores you and build on what draws you back. Broadway doesn't keep on rehearsing plays that are destined to fold before they open. You will know what you like when you try it, but you must try it.

Remember the registered letter you received at the beginning of this step-by-step consideration to help you retire more successfully? No matter which urgent message it contained for you. It did predict and promise that the problems of retirement are going to face you whether you are ready to face them or not. So face them. So rehearse.

There's a charming lady we know who lives in a lakeside community nearby. Her husband is an attorney. The lady paints—beautifully. Professionally. Her paintings are quite in demand at shows throughout the region. She has "one-man shows" regularly, in dozens of larger cities. Each winter she paints up a storm. Her shows each spring and summer are new and fresh—with enough of the evolutionary artistic development she seeks.

This painting lady has other spokes to her own wheel of good fortune. She has been organizing traveling gallery shows, bringing together paintings, prints and graphics from the collections of others and from her own. Each year she and her husband go to Europe to shop for the new works of promising new younger painters. These they buy, originals and prints, building substantial collections. I have often

REHEARSE BEFORE YOU RETIRE 53

imagined that she acquires some of these works for her friends' collections as well. She brings this exciting art for showing in her area. Many of these shows are tied in with summer festivals for showing to vacation visitors. Visitors buy paintings and exhibitors sell—and the wheels of this process churn happily all over again.

I don't know anything about the economics of this procedure. One can imagine that there is great pleasure in the process. There may even be a modest profit—or a break-even result. It is likely that all this energy and effort offers sufficient rewards—or perhaps a promise—whether that be immediate or long range. It keeps on happening and the collections get bigger and better.

Meanwhile, she keeps painting, and collecting. She isn't any more retired than her husband. I have observed that he keeps a business eye on things and together they have this fun and this unfolding excitement which appears also to be filled with many kinds of promise.

Begin by rehearsing for your retirement. Find something that's fun for you—to do regularly—and hopefully for a long time.

ACTION IDEAS TO THINK ABOUT:

- *Can I, and will I, now begin to face the fact that I will be retired? Can I face it with hope?*

    _____
    _____

REHEARSE BEFORE YOU RETIRE

- *Am I still postponing planning—or even thinking about—being retired some day?*

- *What do I fear most—about retirement?*

- *Instead of just retiring, would I rather stay on; phase out over some period; switch to a part-time job; change careers; or begin a new avocational activity—perhaps in a field that's new, too?*

- *Are such choices available; are they apt to be?*

- *What will I now decide to do—about getting ready for my retirement?*

2

Prepare to Retire <u>to</u> Something

RETIREMENT deserves better than to be just the caboose on the life-long freight we have been pulling and hauling mightily. Rather, it should be the engine of enthusiasm that powers us happily toward life's newest and most attractive way stations.

Retirement may come toward the end of our working days, but it's a lot more fun if we think of it as a beginning. A beginning of a whole new timetable of happy and exciting journeys to new places. To meet new people. To accomplish new things.

Far too many families resist retirement as if it were a one-way ticket to doomsday. As if it were the dustiest, weariest flat-car that ever trailed life's longest train.

The experiences of others can often demonstrate alternatives most dramatically.

Two men I know well were sentenced into

Time and Time Again

The one sure gift retirement brings is more time; more free time. You must have something to get up for each and every day or that time may not seem so blessed.

*Here's a typical week of seven days × 24 hours:

HOURS PER WEEK

ACTIVITY	BEFORE Retirement	AFTER Retirement
Working at job	40	0**
Commuting to and from job	10	0**
Sleeping	56	56
Being with the family	21	25
Recreation and resting	16	42
Watching TV and reading	11	20
Doing jobs around the house	10	15
Church and community activities	4	10
TOTAL:	168	168

The one retirement reward all receive equally, each day, is time. ***How are you going to re-harness some of those new-found bonus hours (50 or more hours of free time?)*

*Excerpted in part from: RETIREMENT REHEARSAL GUIDEBOOK

REHEARSE BEFORE YOU RETIRE

their retirement by widely differing judges. Listen to each tell his own story:

Tim tells his tale first. Tiredly. Tim always sounded tired. I often suspected that it was his attitude rather than work that weighed him down so heavily.

"You know I'm retiring in October? Yes sir. Looking forward to it too. Fellow has to enjoy life a little. Fellow sure earns it—after forty years of working hard."

That was in July. I didn't see Tim again until the next April or May. "Been gone four months," Tim reported. "That's why you didn't see us around."

(Pause and sigh)

"Guess you knew I retired in October. We've been in Arizona. They say it's best for climate. For my wife's arthritis. Too hot there now. Over 100 degrees most days."

"How did we like it? Okay I guess."

(Pause and sigh)

"Nothing to do. Never had any hobbies. Never cared much for meeting new people. What's a fellow to do with himself—day after day?

Sure, we've got enough money but that doesn't make the days any shorter—or happier. The Missus likes it okay. Glad she feels good.

Me—I've got nothing to do!" Poor Tim.

Nothing to do. That's quite an assignment to take along into retirement.

It's the poorest kind of program and totally unnecessary. Regardless of one's circumstances. Circumstances represent more than money, more than exciting hobbies, more than a new career, more than just loafing and enjoying life.

Our circumstances include all of our personal resources of which the greatest values are the attitudes and the appetites we bring along into our retirement time of life.

Contrast Tim's tired and empty experience with that of a different kind of guy named Harry.

Planning for retirement is like getting ready to go on a picnic—for some people. Those who give it that kind of happy attention will probably make a picnic out of it.

I think Harry had about the best "picnic preparation program" I've ever heard of. It may have happened to him accidentally, but Harry surely knows how to turn accidents into joyful happenings.

Harry spent five years deciding when and how to retire. Then one day he quit his job. But since my friend Harry brags so well, his telling of his own tale may be best. Hear Harry:

"After 30 years on the same sort of job, day after day, I got fed up with the dull and dreary sameness. Thought I'd never make it to pension day. My wife sent me to the doctor to check up on everything—including my attitude.

"When I had finished spilling my story to the doc, I was tired all over agin. I told him that I was becoming wearier and more irritated day after day from trudging grudgingly around my 15-block mail route. Listening to the same boring complaints. The same puny jokes about the weather or the condition of the world. The same sour sarcasm about how rich I was getting or how poor I was looking.

"After the doctor was thoughtfully quiet for a while he told me that I needed to make some changes.

"Look, Doc, bored I may be, but rich I ain't. I can't change much because I don't have much to change with. I'm locked in by my lousy lot in life.

"Then this doc gave me a strange but delightful prescription.

"He gave it to me after he had heard me recite exactly what I did each day on my route. What I looked at. What I saw that interested me as I made my weary way day after day. I lumped all that I saw into one big heap of crummy buildings, of soured people full of tired crankiness about how "it looks like rain or looks like it won't rain."

"Never any positive "it might be a nice day" comments.

"The doc asked how much longer I had until retirement. I considered it a ridiculous question and told him it was too darned long.

"The doctor suggested that I stop dwelling on all that dreariness. He told me to begin noticing instead the upstairs floors of the stores and buildings along my route. You know what? I discovered an entirely new world up there! A whole new city, largely unexplored.

"And that's where I also found new ideas for my retirement. I adopted a new awareness and a happier attitude and it helped to take the drudgery out of each daily trudge around my route. I also found half a dozen retirement job ideas and finally selected one I liked best.

"In that second story world—in that upstairs Utopia—I found new people, new enterprises and new opportunities for tired old me. They weren't really new but they surely were new to me. I made new friends because of my new attitude. It was fun once again to tackle each day. I was also hunting happily in that newly-discovered land for some choice among a variety of retirement ideas.

"The half dozen part-time job opportunities I picked up as I explored my new upstairs world had probably also been available on the ground floor. But I had long ago despaired of ever getting in on anyone's ground floor.

"I began to moonlight on one or two of the things I discovered and picked up a little extra money. I also picked up a renewed excitement to which I had imagined myself immune. I began testing which of these part-time job replacements I might wish to concentrate on when I was ready to do it full time.

"Would you believe I didn't have to take all those years until my scheduled retirement?

REHEARSE BEFORE YOU RETIRE 61

"Those walkup wonderlands turned up, in the five fruitful years of my apprenticeship, plenty of part-time opportunities from which I was able to pick and choose both the time and conditions of my retirement. Five years earlier than had been prescribed.

"I was able to take an abbreviated pension, to salvage my sanity and retire at 55. The half days of work I am enjoying now satisfy my need for challenge and responsibility and provide almost as much income as I had previously earned full-time. If I'm not careful, I may turn out to be so good at this job that I may find myself working full time again.

"You'll have to excuse my ego and enthusiasm. I wouldn't want you to think I was bragging. But I did quit at 55. The life we lead now provides sufficient dollars and makes a lot more sense. Not for everyone maybe—but for me. Ask the Missus." That's Harry's happy story.

Contrast between the life and times of all the Tims and Harrys.

Between arriving at 65 totally devoid of resilience and human resources. Or chucking it all at 60, or even 55, to begin again to build in a new way, to sprinkle some joy and worth onto the work and worry of the world.

Fortunately most of us are not exactly like either of these two extremes. Our situations vary. Our psychic needs differ—and so do our daily needs.

IF THERE is a message in these anecdotes, it has to do with planned preparation for happier and more satisfying retirement. This surely seems more desirable than to be scared in advance about the reality of being out of work and out of ideas on how to enjoy this new freedom.

For most of us retirement seems a long way off. It is probably an abstract target we cannot quite see and can only inadequately imagine. On good days we may yearn for the time when we can take on new tasks, travel to new places, spend more time at ease. Reading more, fishing more, golfing more. To dream deliciously day after day.

On poor days we may fret about our struggles, our too thin bank account, our weary mind and muscles—or our uncertain health. We think that we may not make it to that elusive far-off time, and if we do, we will probably arrive there as doddering dolts—a pleasure to no one including ourselves.

The hard facts are that many good people like ourselves do retire every year. Most of them do enjoy it. What we are examining here is how to build in some extra insurance for the higher levels of enjoyment which come to those with the vision and the verve to prepare.

To prepare to retire *to* something. Not to retire *to* Arizona or any other specific place as much as to retire *to* something to do. Something to enjoy,

REHEARSE BEFORE YOU RETIRE 63

to accomplish, to learn—something to share. To do something new and probably even important.

The changes that come with retirement will face everyone eventually. It seems better to face such changes now while we can still do something to prepare for them. That's why we will keep suggesting the making of lists of your goals. Setting objectives. Building bridges for crossing later. People we have researched suggest that simple tests helped them in the setting of their goals.

We have devised such a test for you. Try to answer each question from the point of view of your own circumstances. Intellectually honest answers are best. From these questions and your search for answers you will determine what still needs doing to help you get ready better for your retirement.

TEST YOUR OWN RETIREMENT READINESS

How Ready are You for Retirement?
1. *When* would you like to retire?
    a. What age will you be then?
    b. What age will your wife be?
    c. How many years is that from now?
    d. Will anything foreseeable prevent your retiring then?
    e. Is there anything you can do about it now?
2. *Where* would you like to retire to?
    a. Is there any family pressure to prevent it?
    b. Will climate be a problem to you there?

    c. Have you ever tested living there—on vacations?
    d. Are you cottage or apartment people? Or don't you care?
    e. Will you expect to rent or own your home?
3. *Will you have sufficient resources* for enjoying your retirement?
    a. Could you adapt to living on less money?
    b. Will you need to earn some extra money?
    c. Do you already know how you will earn it?
    d. Have you checked out pensions, social security, medicare, other retirement income and welfare helps?
4. *What* will you be doing in retirement?
    a. Will you be totally uninterested in working?
    b. Does a new job or new challenge interest you?
    c. Will retirement changes bother your wife?
    d. Might she take a job—for the fun of it or for the money?
    e. Are either of you apt to be bored?

    The answers you and your wife agree on after this readiness test should show what you still have left to do to make sure you become better prepared—before you retire. Face the facts of retirement before you find them facing you.

    After you have established your retirement objectives, after having taken tests to determine how ready you are, it might be wise to examine alternatives. It's a good idea to increase the certainty that you will have enough of everything—including enough of those attitudes and appetites successful retirees keep mentioning—to last for ten, fifteen or twenty years or more.

Many people who work very hard, and who have often postponed personal pleasures in favor of their work syndrome, yearn to retire. They say they want to fish. To hunt, golf or loaf. Nothing wrong with any of these aims. Some do it and enjoy it. Others, who have led tremendously active lives may think they want to live on the lakes or the links but later find they are no longer patient or serene enough for such an unhurried pace, for such a constant calendar of "fun."

Take fishing. You have to live near the areas where fishing is available. This may not be possible for a lot of people. You have to have equipment and the strength and know-how to use it. If it's good fishing country, there is also a variety of bad weather to reckon with. "Or the wind is from the East when fish bite the least. Or from the North when smart fishermen don't venture forth. Or you should have been here last week—they were really biting then." Does your wife like to fish? Would you enjoy eating all the fish you might catch—in great quantities?

Fishing's great fun—one of nature's nicest presents to him who relishes such peaceful solitude interrupted only by the promise of action on the line.

Golfers tell me they finally weary of trying to bring their handicap down. So they play with other duffers whose handicaps are already going back up. To do this day after day, week after week, finally palls upon them, many say. In the 365 days in any year, if one works at it, one ought to be able to fill freezers with fish—or to bring golf handicaps down respectably. We're told it doesn't quite work out that way. That fishing, golfing and hunting skills and satisfactions normally return to about the pattern followed during a busy working lifetime.

Loafing—now there's a thing I could be good at. I think?

I have observed countless husband and wife teams terribly busy wasting their time while solving the day's absence of any agenda.

"It'll be time for lunch soon and we haven't been to the supermarket yet."

"Which store do you want to shop at today?"

"Depends on what you want to eat. What would you like today?"

"Anything at all. As long as it's different from what we had yesterday."

Or listen to a more financially favored couple setting their daily objectives.

"Where do you want to eat tonight, dear?"

"It doesn't matter. As long as we don't have to go with the Putneys again. He drinks too much."

"Perhaps, dear, but we can't duck them without good reason. You know how sensitive she is."

"I know how boring *he* is when he is full of

REHEARSE BEFORE YOU RETIRE

flit. We still haven't decided where to go to eat tonight."

Amusing exaggeration? Perhaps, but also the truth. Listen as you look about in areas where retired people retire. Listen to their often dreary dialogue as they grind still another day away. Bored stiff!

Fortunately, many happy retired people have better personal resources. They make better plans. They work to accomplish something. To give something back to the world. Or to get still another new experience from it. Those who have no plan probably deserve their tiresome existence. It could be in not knowing how—or in being afraid to face the choice of futures that retirement offers to most anyone.

Perhaps it's the retirement failures which turned me into a nut on making lists—and plans. Lists about retiring *to* something. Urgent jobs that need doing by someone—by some retiree with the experience. Jobs which United Nations committees know and have lists about. Other kinds of people-related jobs which the folks in the world's religious missions know so much about. They have lists too. Long lists of unfinished human business that demand help and action. The kind of urgent jobs we face in this country among our underprivileged, our poor and our handicapped. You won't shy away from getting involved with these people once you have tasted the joyful satisfaction of being involved with them. Others say that this is so.

In any community, large or small, there are urgent tasks in education, in health and welfare, in community service jobs that go begging for lack of people with time and talent. You will have the time—and you have whatever talents you have. Take your pick of the jobs you know about that need doing. The kinds of jobs you would like to help with. If you lack the imagination to make your own choice, go to the people in charge of such needs. Their lists are long indeed. Ask the reference people in your libraries. Read about human need and respond from your heart—with your hands, with time and talent.

No job you have ever had in your working lifetime will match the satisfaction you will find, the fulfillment you will achieve if you take on the kinds of tasks that help by bringing another human being someone to talk to, someone to sit with. Often this is all that is needed but it is a lot. Someone to write letters or to read a poem, a story from a book—or to re-read old letters. To teach simple, helpful and ordinary things to the simple folks who still overflow our midst.

Prepare to retire *to* something.

If altruism doesn't drive you just yet, don't worry about it. You'll find your way of helping and sharing. Perhaps your own work weariness calls for a happier target. Like developing your skills in an

REHEARSE BEFORE YOU RETIRE

appealing hobby. You may be creative—wanting more time to paint, to act in plays, to write or perform music. To take part in your industry's trade shows in order to repay some of the successful working lifetime rewards your industry has provided for you.

There are dreams to dream that haven't yet crossed the mind of men. There just have to be! The world is so full of unsolved problems and unanswered questions that it would seem a tremendous retirement avocational objective might be to set about the job of finding some of those answers or to learn what some of the questions are. To help solve some of those problems—or at least to examine and understand what makes them such problems.

Project planning lists can be long and many. They are available in libraries, at colleges, at consulates to which one may go or write. A little imagination and a little initiative will pay big dividends.

I am indebted to a preacher I have never met who wrote some years ago in a religious magazine published by his church about "A Town Called Service City." My indebtedness concerns the wonderful way in which he dramatized an idea I have been working on with my friends for a long time. It's the very simple, and probably somewhat selfish proposition, that you yourself can get your biggest kicks by helping other people. By helping them to smile, to love and to share from out of themselves.

It would amaze a lot of self-sufficient people

to learn how many, many people are lonely—whether they are with others or not. How many people are all alone a lot of the time. Most can't do anything about their circumstance any more. They are too old, too tired, too unwell—or too filled with the negative habit of introspection and self-pity.

Here's another helping-hand list—from the People-to-People program. Things anyone can do. The People-to-People program suggests many opportunities—like calling high schools or colleges for the names of exchange students so that you can invite them to your home. So that they may get to know more Americans and that you may have the opportunity of getting to know some of those from strange lands who visit here. It's important for us to learn of their pride in their own heritage.

The People-to-People program can also help provide names of families with whom you can correspond in other countries. To whom you can send magazine or newspaper articles about our country, to be read and passed on. Think of the monumental waste of the unread and un-reread books we leave on dusty shelves, to be retired to attics—eventually to be discarded.

People-to-People suggests getting acquainted with foreign visitors who come to your town. It's easy to arrange to meet them by contacting the hotels where they normally stay, by checking with plants they normally visit or schools they are usually entertained at. Wouldn't it be fun to make a new

REHEARSE BEFORE YOU RETIRE 71

friend from a new country—and even to agree to visit him in his native home another day?

Meeting foreign-born American neighbors is another good way to learn of the many homelands with which we may not be very familiar. Most of these people speak our language but most remember and cherish their former homeland's customs. They have national pride and often a different point of view. They can help us understand those things which are different elsewhere.

Anyone can study a little of any foreign language. The study of language may not be easy. But it is not impossible to learn some words to use with foreign visitors. Especially to use such words and phrases if one should be visiting abroad.

Advice from the Portuguese Embassy for example included the simple suggestion that my wife and I learn just a few words of Portuguese before visiting there. We were assured that it will prove that we care about them and about their heritage. "We will all love you for it, no matter how poorly you may say the words," was his promise.

But we have wandered away from "A Town Called Service City."

I seem to recall that it was either a vision or a dream. Our preacher friend was not sure. It could have been a reality. Service City was a place where people retired—to help each other and to help other people. They had projects that turned energy and enthusiasm into a little money for causes which abound everywhere. Help with driver training, teaching backward students, encouraging those who were underprivileged. Helping with nursing care in homes where aged and infirm languish in loneliness. The companionship of a game of checkers. A spirited game of shuffleboard. Playing instruments to provide music for a dance. Or simply to dance!

Most of us need not take any great new steps in order to prepare to retire *to* something. We all have in the backs of our minds neglected objectives and forgotten goals. The time is now to haul them out, to dust them off and to plan our next steps.

Far be it for "this preacher" to propose that the only way to get the most out of retirement is to become a first-class do-gooder. That's just one way! It's an important way that has appeal for many and it can indeed be a worthwhile goal for many more. There are those, however, who would rather set other goals, to be off in search of other rewards. Whether the goals are for love or money is not the point of this particular message. The point is rather that there be a goal.

You're a lot more exciting as a person if you're an expert on something. People listen to experts. They'll seek you out and ask your advice. Become an expert. Build on what has been your life's work. Add a dash of distinction, enough to spice up yourself and your area of expertise.

Become a new expert in a field that is new to you. It's done every day. A man I know liked to visit

REHEARSE BEFORE YOU RETIRE

with people. His father had been a carpenter and he himself had been a veterinarian. Now that he was retiring, he wondered how he might put together the best of the three worlds of his experience? Our man studied and read a lot. He talked to many people. He equipped himself with new skill and new knowledge. He took out the necessary license to become a pest control expert. He knew something about homes and structures from his carpenter father. He knew about "wild life" from his days of doctoring sick livestock. He knew that people have pest problems. He put them all together and had an important and needed service at which he now works. He makes appointments by telephone for as much time as he wants to work. He's making about as much money as he had averaged while he labored away in his fulltime lifetime as a sawbones to sick country cattle.

Once when I was getting sunburned beside a pool in Puerto Rico I overheard a well-fed, cigar-smoking tycoon from up north tell his seemingly indifferent wife while she was spreading sun tan lotion all over his broad back that he had just noticed in the WALL STREET JOURNAL that he had made $2,000 the day before. One assumes that he had bought the right stock at the right price at the right time. His wife shrugged without interrupting her massage to say simply and dispassionately that he would probably be losing it again tomorrow. Some of us might be fortunate enough to play in the majors like this but the rest of us happily take our turn at bat in littler leagues.

We have been examining the subject of retiring *to* something without regard to where it is you want to retire. It does not seem to matter where you wish to live from the standpoint of what you can do there. Usually either the husband or wife—or both—can find something in the way of gainful employment whether in full-time or part-time work.

Substitute teachers, preachers, librarians—you name it—they're in frequent demand. Part-time sales clerks normally find a variety of part-time work opportunities. Jobs in retirement may depend on your life's work experience. They might grow out of hobbies or special studies which have interested you.

It is important to remember that retirement is a different way of life. There is usually less income available—and more time in which to enjoy the things that money might buy.

Fortunately when people retire they have probably also arrived at a time when their appetites for enjoyment have cooled off a bit. Fiscal preparation, the dollars and "sense" part of retirement reality, is another subject and will be treated in another way at another time. We are examining here now the things you might do, the things you might retire *to*.

In all this enthusiastic dialogue about all the things one might do in the days of his retirement, we keep forgetting that some people don't want to do much at all.

REHEARSE BEFORE YOU RETIRE

I met such a man recently at a country club in one of those Southern retirement communities which are springing up to bring the delightful advantages of sea, sun and sand to many who have not enjoyed them before. This man appeared not to be working very hard—if he was working at all. I fell into conversation with him and asked whether he was a retired businessman from the north.

"Nope, I was a farmer. Upper New York state. About 15 miles from Canada. Tough to make it on a dairy farm today. High costs, low milk income. I couldn't take it any more."

"Trouble with your health?"

"A little—in my shoulders and arms."

"Did you come down here to buy one of those by-the-planeload-prospect-party homesites? Did you get talked into one of those retirement homes? Did you come here to take it easier? How old are you?"

"That's a lot of questions. I'm just 60. We came to look at those homes, but we bought ours from a regular real estate dealer, not from the land corporation. Nothing wrong either way, mind you. Matter of fact I've since bought another lot. As an investment. Like I say, I couldn't take it up north so we came here to take it easier, where it's warmer. Where the sun shines and where the work is easier."

He was sitting on one of those electric golf carts and I wondered if he was skylarking—or working. So I asked him:

"You work here?"

"Used to work in the kitchen, but the steam in the dishwasher and the detergent dust got to my breathing. So I quit. Now I'm the golf cart jockey here at the country club. I'm used to engines and equipment like this. Help keep it in order and when the pro assigns one I get it to the golfers and when they're finished, put them back into their storage garage. It's not much of a job. It's not too much money. But it's the kind of thing I can do and like to do. Like I say, it's not much but it's exactly what I want. Not much."

Glen Paxter was his name. He didn't tell me directly but I thought that he seemed concerned about a heart problem, or a lung thing or something. Anyway, I was impressed that he was exactly where he wanted to be, doing exactly what he wanted to do—not much.

I asked Mr. Paxter how he found this type of low-pressure job. He said this particular land corporation had an employment service to provide people to fill its wide variety of needs. He said that there were also temporary help agencies where one could register—listing skills, including things like typing, accounting, engineering, selling and many others. The agencies give simple tests which pinpoint abilities and relate skills to requests they have for help. Often, hobby skills relate even more directly to employment in these situations than regular work skills do. After all, we have been examining job opportuni-

REHEARSE BEFORE YOU RETIRE 77

ties in relaxation centers. Why not put hobby skills to work—for fun *and* profit.

Lots of people who have never been self-employed think it would be fun to go into business when they retire. For some it has turned out to be just what the doctor ordered. With a great deal of study and care, it is possible to find small businesses to purchase. By an even more careful investigation—with the help of experts it's wise to call in—one is usually able to sort out the poor deals from the better situations. If one is terribly naive and inexperienced one should probably not yearn to "get into a business of my own."

A MODERN day phenomenon that fits many energetic retiring persons is the growing field of franchising. Here's a good place to make haste slowly. There are good chances of making money by joining reputable franchising firms in doughnut operations, chicken huts or hamburger haciendas. From among the multitude of franchise opportunities now available, I just spotted another new one. This one sells pies—home-baked pies. How's this for a sales slogan? "Mother bakes the pies before your very eyes."

Franchising apparently systematizes materials costs, labor costs, location and rental costs—and all other overhead and costs. Notice the emphasis on costs. Best if you notice it in advance. Costs are always present in business. Success depends on how much you can exceed costs with volume and take-home profit. It's being done happily and profitably by many.

Sometimes the gain comes from owning and not operating—leaving that task to other, more robust and younger types. Sometimes, in smaller operations, the work can be done by a couple. But make no mistake, the work isn't easy. If there is a reward, if there is profit to be made, there must also be risk. Risk and reward seem to be the irrevocable Siamese-twin law of the land of private enterprise.

There's no need here to make this into a litany of job and business opportunities. Our only purpose is to examine the many pathways to pleasant, prosperous and satisfying retirement years. Our task is to find ideas and ways to help people prepare to retire *to* something.

Where in the world have you visited over the years? Where have you most enjoyed vacationing? Where do your children live? Where are your grandchildren?

Would you like to live there? Are there sufficiently interesting things to see and do? Are there facilities for study, for you to learn and grow if that should be your bent?

What might you do there? Are there tasks that you would want to take on—that you could help with doing? Do you have either specific—or general—help to bring to the needs existing in any of these places? Do you have hobbies to perfect, to share and to enjoy? Will you have enough money to do what

REHEARSE BEFORE YOU RETIRE

you want? Or will you be faced with the necessity of acquiring some extra, new money? Can you invest or have you little more than your own personal interest to invest?

What skills have you to share, to teach, to profit from? Can you find people to serve, to comfort, to learn from?

Do you have curiosities that need satisfying? Are you the type that likes to think new ideas, to create? Do you have stored-up ideas to develop? Are you expert enough to find satisfying work and pleasure in writing or speaking on subjects in which you excel?

Retirement days need not be filled with this many leftover questions—especially if you take time now to ask and answer them.

One simple but important word of warning. Try as well as you can to determine whether your dreams for retirement are attainable goals. Whether they are realistic enough to promise reasonable realization. Beware of being an impractical escapist. Try to sift out the dreamy dreams from the delightful realities.

A pertinent cartoon ran some years ago in a farm publication and it showed how very much like mankind cattle can be. The picture showed a cow down on her front knees with her head through the wire fence eating away at the grass from the adjoining field. The next panel showed the cow rising, looking around, finding a gate open and walking through it. Now what did she do? In the last panel the cow was once again down on her knees, head thrust through the fence, joyfully eating the grass from the original side from whence she had come. No need to caution you against this grass is greener syndrome. In some ways it's probably fortunate that the grass does appear greener in other pastures. It keeps us reaching. Keeps us trying, investigating, sampling and growing.

In this preparation for retiring *to* something, some greener pastures can be pertinent and helpful. You'll find soon enough that the world of retired people is filled with tale after tale about just how it is for those other people. How everybody knows that Tuesday is when the Snyders get their pension check. And how much it is. And how his arthritis is worsening And how maybe she drinks a little—when she's alone. What's different about retired people? It's just another universe.

Probably the biggest reality retired people have in common is that they are no longer as young as they used to be. Beyond that, they share all the variety of the rest of the human race. Except that most of them don't work as much as they used to.

When we talk about retiring *to* something we are not saying that you must find gainful employment. That you must be busy doing something, running somewhere, solving the world's problems.

Unless that's what you want to do. There's the key. What do you want to do?

REHEARSE BEFORE YOU RETIRE

"I don't want to be bored. That's one thing I don't want to be."

How can one insure against being bored? We've all heard them tell it. One week after getting their gold watch, the color TV set or the letter from the president, they're telling everyone "I'm so busy since I retired. I don't know how I ever had time for my job." "There simply aren't enough hours in the day to take care of all of the things I must do."

Such a recitation of how this awful, over-busy retired syndrome goes would be too boring for you to read—and too arduous for me to set down. It's the song of an often lazy man with a lazy mind.

Believe the facts. Many retired men are very busy indeed and many retired couples happily keep very busy.

But there's a big difference between being really busy—and being really big time wasters and time killers.

An activity log of one dreary day after another in the lives of so many of these people is indeed a great sadness to those who covet time for what can be done with it. For the goals you can climb toward—things you want to accomplish and enjoy. True, some people are low in activity energy, probably also low in psychic energies and in intellectual curiosity. But our program calls for you to do what you can now to prepare so that you will have something to do when you are retired—to retire *to* something.

You have worked hard and dreamed long of the time when the harness could hang more loosely and the horizons could be more varied. You deserve your opportunity to pick from among the fruits in the garden—one sunny day after another. Be assured that life isn't exactly like that. But it can be somewhat like that for many of you.

Don't forget, they need you in "a town called Service City."

If your bent is to serve—to serve others.

But, if instead you wish to serve yourself, think of all the ways in which you might join the Glen Paxters, sitting astride a golf cart at a sun-soaked tropical country club facing gulf, the greensward or the ocean. Housing that's paid for. Health that's being preserved. A little money being made to be used pleasantly and practically. It's not a bad kind of life for a lot of us. We've gotten used to beating ourselves over the head without ever really learning to enjoy it half as much as we kept saying we do.

The question has been raised before. Can you teach? Or do you preach? There's a law school—Hastings in California—that hires for its faculty principally attorneys who have passed retirement age. Men who have made their mark in jurisprudence. Men who have specialized in various phases of the law. Seems that I remember one of them was 81—or even older. The idea is compelling.

I'll bet that's no rest home for law students

either. With the fiery vigor of a lifetime of appealing cases, representing clients, effecting settlements, planning estates, counseling corporations, protecting the unwary and representing those who become entangled. It's a job that needs doing and who can do it better than the people who have spent their successful lifetime having and demonstrating such skills? I'll bet it's exciting work teaching there. I'll bet also that it's exciting being a student there.

Colleges and universities are exploding into more adult-oriented continuing education. They report being short of special skill teaching and life's experience instructors. Lots of men we know are joining faculty ranks and more will do it just as soon as the bugaboos of "teaching tenure" and pensions get resolved. These new people don't expect to move in on all those privileged domains as much as they want the chance to share their skill, to excite excitable students, to counsel, to guide and to stir the potential of an increasingly brighter and tougher minded young audience. Spreading the ideas which can help mankind here and abroad. Let them teach. Let them preach. They'll find the way to do it. It's about as worthwhile as anything you've ever done.

A word of solace to those who have not been lifetime job hunters. In your zeal to share, to find a job, to buy a business, to become a teacher, to do anything you are not presently doing, don't let the first gum-chewing, uninvolved, bored and dull receptionist in the XYZ offices of the world discourage you. Don't let them grind you down with their indifference. Their world needs exactly you but they're too lazy or too burned out at 20 to get the message you're trying to bring to their sleepy Garcias.

This is no attack on all the wonderful young people who man the front desks of the world. But if one has traveled and made lots of calls one has found a kind of unimaginative and uninvolved front line that must be hurdled by the persevering. Best way to guarantee that you're going to get through on anything important is to write a note to the secretary of the busy man you want to see. Tell her you're going to call her for an appointment with him. It works. Or call directly for an appointment—especially in the larger cities where each day is segmented into little slices of now-you-have-me and next-he-gets-me and where-the-hell-am-I-due-at-three-o'clock?

If you have a plan, if you are preparing for something, if you get it outlined and written, place it in a neat presentation jacket like lawyers and advertising men use. If they can turn their thoughts and ideas into big dollars, you also can get in almost anywhere and reach almost anyone—with plans that demonstrate planning.

Just be sure that you know why he should care about you and your ideas. Perhaps he's the wrong guy. Perhaps yours is the wrong idea at the wrong time—for him. Don't despair. Hone it more sharply. Develop it further. Take it to someone else.

REHEARSE BEFORE YOU RETIRE

You say you would like to sell something. Go ahead and sell—yourself. Tell about your needs. Your psychological needs. Your practical needs. Tell it positively and personally. You say you have a need for money for retirement. Most people have some of that need. And yet a very large number of people will end up in retirement without enough ideas about how most intelligently to use the resources and the money they do have. It will take a little work, but it can be figured out better by most people. Tell that you have special skills, some singular know-how, some unusual knowledge to share, to apply. You may even have some special insights or unusual talent to bring to bear on a specific problem in a specific place during your retirement years. Most of us have something singular to offer. But most of us are rather poor at marketing or finding the way to share these needed attributes.

One thing you can be quite sure of. There are an almost uncountable number of people out there in your forthcoming retirement world who need exactly what it is you have to share. Something to teach, to help with or to lovingly join in passing a happier time of day. This is true in every hamlet, in any state. None escapes this abundance—if it can be called an abundance. There is indeed an abundance of needs—needs to match our own clamor to be heard and to be helpful.

FINALLY, ask yourself just one more question,

after all of the questions which retirement preparation has been asking of you.

"What would you most like to do when you retire?"

Mind you now, what would *you* most like to do during the years you will have left to enjoy, with or without a spouse, with or without a lot of money, with or without a lot of talent and skill, with or without unusual insights into how to harness and how to bring your needs to the attention of your new world.

What would *you* most like to do in your own retirement?

There is a fine old clergyman who managed a somewhat early retirement in his diocese in midwestern America. We met him in one of the Bahama Islands. He stopped us for a visit after service on Sunday.

He appeared to be just a touch hungry for a visit with "someone who looked like home." That may have been part of his purpose in stopping us. Perhaps it was just his fatherly attitude toward his flock. We were visitors for just that Sunday.

This "retired" church man of about 70 was delightedly telling and showing us how he was turning an old garage into a church for his new and growing congregation. But his flock didn't seem to be too well-feathered. I gathered that the Reverend had a tough task keeping his bodies and his souls together.

REHEARSE BEFORE YOU RETIRE 87

You may be sure that his name and address and ours were handily exchanged that Sunday morning. And you may be sure that he has heard from us and that we have heard from him, often, about his progress, his problems, his beloved flock and his poor, poor people and his poor, poor parish.

And how the winds blew and the rains came and how he needs more friends like us. He and his kind also need friends just like you. And you perchance can help him more and in better ways than has been our privilege.

Fathom the future of this 70-year old pastor, happy as a schoolboy—retired to a terrifying and delightful new challenge. Where people really need him. They know it and he knows it. And they love each other because each is serving the other.

What had "our Shepherd" done—back in his native diocese to help him become so lucky? If luck it is—to be the poor pastor of a poor, inadequately-feathered flock.

We talked with him about this and he gave us the same answer we have been trying to share with you.

He told in detail how, in his later pastoral life, he had prepared to retire *to* something. He had set a retirement goal—one with a high and happy purpose. And this new and native flock and their poor new church were his very special *something*.

For they were what he had retired *to*.

REHEARSE BEFORE YOU RETIRE

ACTION IDEAS TO THINK ABOUT:

Use this Retirement Activity Selection Guide to focus on your best and most preferred retirement activities:

1. List educational history and what this prepared you to do—even beyond your life's work experience.

   _____
   _____
   _____
   _____

2. List best jobs; work experiences you had and enjoyed.

   _____
   _____
   _____
   _____

3. List spare time (hobbies, other) skills and activities.

   _____
   _____
   _____
   _____

4. List special study or primary hobby in which you may be a recognized and considerable expert.

   _____
   _____
   _____

5. Select from these the two, three or more very best activities you prefer—and are best at. Eliminate minor interests or marginal aptitudes—unless you wish now to develop such new skill and knowledge.

   _____
   _____
   _____
   _____

3

Establish Sensible Retirement Expectations

WHEN it comes to questions like: whom to marry, how to invest money or what to do and where to do it in retirement—everybody's an expert. Especially relatives.

Everybody will be lucky if he can truly be his own expert. Nobody can be your authority on this matter half as well as you can.

Who's retiring anyway?

Let's do a simple one-question quiz to find the answer. Think of this question as being projected on your own TV screen—on a program prepared and presented just for you. Think of it as a big poster in your local postoffice with your own picture and with the word "wanted" at the top. Think of it as a test *you* must take in order to graduate from your own particular kind of grind. The question:

Are You Ready to Slay These Dragons?

You can make your retirement into a real reward—or turn it into an empty disappointment. The majority of retirees have pretty good luck with these realities—by facing them.

A. HEALTH:

  How well do you know your body?_____
  Do you understand how to relax?_____
  Does nutrition figure in your eating?_____
  Can you hold tight to good attitudes?_____

B. MONEY:

  Does money remain a worry dilemma to you?_____
  How worried are you about becoming
    dependent?_____
  Does cost of health care—being sick
    bother you?_____
  Do you expect to leave some money to others?____

C. LONELINESS/BOREDOM:

  Afraid of being lonely—or bored?_____
  Do you expect to be any lonelier than others?_____
  Know anybody (several perhaps) who may
    need you?_____
  Will you try to get interested in others?_____

D. WHERE TO LIVE:

  Know exactly where you expect to live?_____
  Prefer to stay right where you are?_____
  How vital is simpler/cheaper housing?_____
  Does climate attract—or control—you?_____
  All set—on geographic area?
    on housing type?_____

REHEARSE BEFORE YOU RETIRE

"What Do *You* Expect From *Your* Retirement?"

Retirement ruminations are full of handy-dandy advice on how to do this, do that—don't do this, don't do that. Seldom does anyone ask what *you* want to do, what you want to accomplish. What do you want to enjoy, what do you expect from your own retirement.

It's vital to remind men who are maturing to prepare to retire *to* something. It adds an almost certain guarantee of success for the prospective retiree who will rehearse before he retires. But in the final analysis, nothing can take the place of this question of your expectations, and of the answer you have sensibly set down. Sensible goals help you avoid the kind of childish disappointment one often finds in families who haul their retirement resources in an empty wagon—who arrive in this promised land with Utopian hopes which will surely be quickly shattered.

It must be a touch unreal to expect always to be comfortable, cradled all the way to our grave in this socialized society. But it makes sensible sense to arrive at any picnic—however high your hopes that this will be a pleasant time—looking forward realistically to the possibility of rain, to the presence of ants and to the sting of a few mosquitoes. That's life.

One could quote from any Bible. The admonition remains the same: "Remember the birds of the air and the lilies of the field. Neither do they toil nor spin. Should not you who are greater than these, have an equivalent faith? Worry not about what you shall eat, what you shall wear, how perfect your retirement experience shall be."

Clumsily quoted perhaps, though not irrelevantly, or irreverently. We're after a suitable sentiment to help establish the point that your retirement success will have had a great deal to do—and is greatly dependent upon—the level and limit of your expectations.

Not that you should necessarily expect little. Or nothing. Nothing but empty days and lonely long hours with nothing to do. Our platform rather suggests that you use your assets and your personal resources to structure sensible expectations—and to keep them practical.

Let time tell you the happy story of a happy friend of mine. He and his wife boarded a jet for a month's tour of Scandinavian countries. It was summer there with nothing but pleasant weather. It's always pleasant weather for this honest and happy student of life. His ancestors must have passed on these stalwart Nordic qualities. Including the quality of living a life filled with sensible expectations.

Axel spent his working life in middle management, in a company whose sales and growth prospered mightily. Axel did not become his company's president. Neither was he a minor leaguer there. He lived his life in the middle of life—where most of us are—and he made his mark in the middle. He and

REHEARSE BEFORE YOU RETIRE

his wife had looked forward to retirement and have since spent several years of it traveling to and from visits with their children plus other visits to long-neglected Scandinavian relatives sprinkled around the country. They read much and relate often to a comfortable circle of old and new friends. Neither Axel nor his wife think they will find in their journeys any new answers. They do hope to find substantiation of most of the same good old answers. They expect to be moderately comfortable and mostly pleased with life. On days when it may rain, or when the weather blows, they will shut the shutters and gather before a homey hearth.

This portrait of two people may sound a bit too pat to the skeptical. These people don't lack their own kind of sophistication, but they also possess good sense, good faith and sound expectations.

No one says you have to wait until you are too old in order to begin the process of enjoying.

I once had a young friend who was a dashing young man of the world. He made his mark less in the promotional job which paid his keep than he did by lowering his golf handicap. He cut quite a swath at his country club at the same time. He knew how to keep his head down to keep his score down—except, as he was wont to say, when a breeze-blown skirt went by. He professed to miss a lot of good tee shots because of his windward and wayward eye.

I remember one time sharing foolish philosophies with him. He suggested that the science of society was all turned upside down. He reminded our older friends that here was he with all of the world's appetites and energies—with empty pockets.

And there were our loaded but older friends, their appetites curbed by doctors and worry, with bulging bank accounts and little on which to lavish them that was either exciting, delicious or attainable any more. We agreed with the sporting spirit of this frivolous philosophy—that retirement and the money to enjoy it ought to come earlier to the young. Perhaps as soon as ten years after college. Then they could take advantage of the pleasures of the land which they best knew how to enjoy.

Give them an earlier access to their later lifetime "pile." Let them enjoy their lives and the lives of those whom they might touch. We agreed that all this living it up might prevent them from arriving at an older age, that those who would make it might come there wiser, enriched by the insights of experience, thereby offering their world so much more. Especially more memories.

I am sure there is either something sinister, sinful or wildly socialistic in this whimsical digression. I dare say that most who heard these idle ideas may have thought them silly. None was willing to say he wouldn't like the chance of testing the theory.

It spoils the story only a little to report that our dreamer has already passed on—early in the middle of his life. Our older friends are now much older, probably much wealthier and perhaps even wiser. We remember these yearnful yarns with quiet fun. Who knows who's right? It doesn't matter except to help us point our own way, to help us set our own expectations sensibly.

We worry. "Will there be enough money?" It's a practical question and a real problem for many. For most who will read these words, the problem will not be as acute as our concern. The economy prospers and inflates. In the process it anticipates a piece of what we have piled up for tomorrow. Some of it leaches away. Society also makes progress. Our swelling welfare world plans programs which look after more and more of our individual and family needs. The process goes on with an ever-increasing watchfulness over an ever-increasing number of people who are no longer as young as they once were. We live longer than ever before and have longer later lives in which to enjoy future fruits of life's expectations. At the same time, we have longer in which to be concerned about what we didn't save for all those extra years of rainy days.

But there are new frontiers. Our retirement dollars might not give each of us endless years of roaring around through endless days of pleasure. Should that be the only goal for resources?

A SUCCESSFUL dairyman from Indiana decided to do it a different way. He took a trip into inland Bolivia and found there an abnormal need for his kind of skill and know-how—and for a little of his resources. The government of Bolivia insists upon partnerships between its own people with incoming investors. At the same time, they insist that their people's needs transcend the need for impractical and extreme limitations on such investments. Our Hoosier dairyman found that a relatively modest investment—compounded by added local money from the Bolivian people and from the institutions of that country—permitted the quick establishment of an immediately successful enterprise. For the first time cheese and ice cream have come to these undernourished and underdeveloped people. At the same time, the dairy will commercially produce a popular Bolivian treat called dulce de leche which had previously been made only at home, or had been imported.

It will also provide for the first time, pasteurized milk. These are basic benefits but our Mr. Milk is not dealing in 1968 standards there. You can't begin at the end of our experience. He tells about the state of the Bolivian economy and society and reminds that he is discussing a 1920 level of problem. Simpler measures and a more modest investment provide quicker benefits and quicker answers and ready employment for added Bolivians. They are sensible and practical. He insists that it would have been too costly, too advanced and too economically frightening for either the Bolivians or for himself to have invested in and installed today's level of American dairying sophistication. The project would have been doomed from the start on too many realistic points.

It's added fun to report that our sincerely altruistic dairyman expects to enjoy about a 10 percent return on his investment. With visits to Bolivia not oftener than four times per year, he is comfortably sure of the sincere determination of the Bolivians to see this thing through to a maximum success—together. He is helping a people who welcome his help. He helps himself by establishing future growth where the future is still unlimited. At the same time he is fortunate to be able to put the whole thing on an economic basis. A promising success and a rewarding experience.

Sensible expectations need not all be like the lilies of the field. They just need to be relative to the subject at hand, to the talents we bring, to the resources we have garnered. And, to the needs of reality.

We know another young person who did something about his lot. He was well on his way to the executive dining room and to executive pay in the promotional end of a manufacturing company in the paper business. He and his wife felt they wanted to bring their children up in a somewhat less harried time and place, and at the same time find a more serene and thoughtful life for themselves—to read, to think, ponder and live.

They left security behind and invested their energies and ambitions and their limited resources in a small, expandable motel-type inn which brought to their beautiful resort community innovations and appeals that had not previously abounded there. They worked hard in the early days, building, fixing and maintaining their growing inn. They have since added new wings, more facilities and extra niceties. These include fine paintings on the walls of beautifully decorated rooms where it is a pleasure to linger longer, to pay a little more in order to enjoy a vacation change so much more.

These young folks brought his promotional skills to their new venture. They gambled somewhat heavily on the outcome. It happens that these are reasonable risks for people who know their skills and talents, and who also recognize their limitations. Underfinancing could have done them in. It is the one most prevalent reason for business failure. But they were sensible. They managed and they made it. Now, about 20 years into their project, they are well on their way to having the kind of six month business each season which they enjoy. During the rest of the year they are able to live a less energetic and more enjoyable life. Extra personal time provided and coveted—to be used for the development of other talents and interests. It doesn't sound like a bad way to solve some of the reflective needs of life.

Programs like this are being practiced by many—young and old alike. By people who run northern resorts, motels, other concessions in resort country. Dining places which operate during the season and close when the children return to school. Some of these go South to do the same in another place in another season. Many take their hard-won gains of a hard and busy season to go to gentler climates for their own re-creational regimen. There are so many ways to do these tasks and yet so many ways in which unreal expectations bring them to failure.

One way to make more certain that you will know in advance what to expect is to make check lists—to face both the questions and answers—before you get there.

WHAT DO YOU EXPECT FROM YOUR RETIREMENT?

Q. 1. What will you do in retirement?
A. 1.
Q. 2. What would you like to do?
A. 2.
Q. 3. What several and related things would you enjoy doing most?
A. 3.
Q. 4. What would you like to accomplish in retirement?
A. 4.
Q. 5. What do you think you can accomplish?
A. 5.
Q. 6. What service or benefit would you like to contribute when you retire? To whom?
A. 6.

Q. 7. What have you to contribute—to your neighbor? To society?

A. 7.

Q. 8. What would you like to get out of retirement?

A. 8.

Q. 9. Are you willing and able to put some effort into retirement planning—for greater success?

A. 9.

Q. 10. Which of these questions are altered by certain hard facts of your life?

A. 10.

If you have never traveled to a far land before, it will be difficult to know exactly how things are there. What are the people like? What effect have local customs on our own attitudes and reactions? Retirement living is a land which remains foreign to those who have not been there before.

We cannot be sure what our attitudes will be toward the things we will find there. One way to remove many of the uncertainties, of course, is to go there—beforehand. To rehearse before we retire. To make sure that we have something to retire *to*.

For many men and women, retirement will simply be a changed time with changed circumstance. Little or no everyday work to do. With less income with which to do things. With somewhat lessened energies and appetites. Retirement usually happens in that period of life when we recognize that we aren't as young as we once were. Or as ambitious or hungry for the excitement and the hopped-up pleasures and activities of younger days. It seems sensible, then, to recognize this by planning for a new kind of activity—or for a new lack of so much activity?

The entire business of putting old workhorses out to pasture should carry with it the kindness to grant "old Dobbin" a little peace, some calm and quiet joy. With just about enough food, clothing, and shelter—and sufficient human love and understanding—to make him feel good and pleased with his life. Society should not reject responsible workhorses by treating them like worn out nags. Nor should we expect them to pull heavy loads with any regularity, to run in fast races with younger, more sprightly steeds. Not long ago along the Gulf Coast in Florida I met another man who had what seemed like another part-time job taking care of the customer relations end of still another new golf course. It wasn't exactly a pro shop but it had golfing gear for sale. Neither was it a restaurant, although it had a few items of food and drink convenient for purchase. This retired sales manager was manager of this brand new "pro shop." He was the starter who regulated play. He rented carts and clubs. He sold golf balls and other necessities.

This former office equipment promoter had worked in several northern states in the Midwest. He had made his mark and appeared to have been a success. He retired a year prior to the official 65 to enjoy his substantial pension. He wanted to get started with the business of building a new life for himself and his wife and two college-age sons who were still dependent upon him.

They bought one of the new development properties which boasted a bay for a yacht. Later they found they hadn't needed the boat very much. He and a married daughter claimed to enjoy their swimming pool for a year or two. It stands almost idle now except for special Northern visitors. He laments having to clean the thing. Says he enjoyed having had it but admits he doesn't really need it, or want it, anymore.

This successful businessman and his family changed their lives successfully. He brought with him enough people-contact skills to make him an excellent daily-fee golf course pro shop operator. I forgot to ask how good his own game was. I don't know if he plays any more. But I doubt that such a man had found himself in such a place without having built onto former pastimes.

Why not combine the things we have enjoyed with opportunities we can easily find? Why not make part-time use of familiar skills and attitudes to turn a few dollars, to fill a few hours, to keep us useful, to give us new friends and fellowship—to keep us out underfoot and to help maintain our self-respect?

Increasing service needs throughout America

REHEARSE BEFORE YOU RETIRE

grow by leaps and bounds. Opportunities are unlimited for retired people or for those who would like to retire a bit early. It's possible to find employment with less pressure and more pleasure in pleasant places, in happy climates, among people who are like-minded.

It must be borne in mind that retirement will not be exactly the same as our working life-times. Why should it be? It ought to be a time without driving ambition, except as practical demands require. It should be a time when needs have mostly been met and wants are kept more simple. Retirement is a time of reality and it should be prepared for and accepted with just such expectation.

There are other people in each of our lives who may have something to say about the kind of retirement expectations which will be sensible and practical for us. It is necessary to accept these facts of our lives. Your family may expect you to live in a certain way, in a certain place—according to their demands on you—and according to the way in which their fair demands can be accommodated by you.

Perhaps you will decide for yourself whether your family has a vote in your retirement. By your family we do not mean you and your wife. We mean your children, your brothers and sisters—or even if you are lucky, a parent or parents.

But what do *you* want? Where do you want to go? What will you want to do? For most people, family demands have little influence any more. Welcome their suggestions—but make your own decisions.

Speaking of wives. It is one of life's realities that what one's wife requires for her health, for her well-being and psychological happiness, is indeed a reality that should and must be recognized. One simply can't go into any unacceptable kind of retirement program in which the wife is not happily involved and in which she cannot invest herself sincerely.

Some wives accomodate their wishes to those of their husbands. Some other wives do not.

Some husbands may have missed noticing the time in life when family decision-making patterns were set. It may now be too late to re-do the job. Most wives may need to be convinced that what is best for both of them collectively is the sum total of what is best for each of them individually. The needs of the husband ought to be recognized, but the wishes of the wife cannot be ignored or it won't work well.

It is an obvious truism of retirement living that this is life's poorest time for improving on bickering and disagreement skills. There will now be so much new time in which to work on these abilities— far beyond anyone's appetite. There's more time to disagree so it becomes more important to broaden areas of agreement. To avoid establishing new

REHEARSE BEFORE YOU RETIRE

chances for failure in retirement living. It is truly a together time.

Your doctor may have something to say about your retirement ideas. You and your wife will decide how carefully you will listen to him. It depends on his appraisal of your situation. Whether he knows you well or not. If either you or your wife have conditions that demand a certain kind of climate, a special type of housing (which really ought to be available anywhere), nearness to family for emotional security reasons—or any of a number of other special circumstance prescriptions, then he should be listened to.

If it does not seem to the two of you that your doctor's suggestions are sufficiently urgent, there is always the opinion of another doctor or another clinic which might put your minds at rest. Most of us will not want to fly in the face of the concern of our doctor if he is knowledgeable about our individual or collective cases.

We speak here of psychological and mental health just as much as we do of physical disabilities and normal aches and pains. Today's society will not permit us to ignore the stresses of life which have fallen our way. Many doctors feel that most of us could do a little better about accepting life as it is. Those couples who have something to retire *to*—or those who have been there before and have rehearsed for that good time—will probably come equipped with better expectations and have a better chance that they will be realized.

It's fun to tell the stories of those who have done their preparation well. A couple we met in our travels had a fascinating pastime that surely went beyond hobby proportions. They were nature buffs in the broadest sense, being equally fond of flora and fauna. They were extremely knowledgeable having had the advantages of arboretum training and lectures, with "walks" in mountains and meadows, to hear and see, to observe and learn about all kinds of life and living things.

This couple specialized in butterflies. Monarch butterflies. They bred and raised these butterflies to better observe everything about their life and living—and to provide microscopic photography opportunities for shooting close-up color slides. They built a library of color film for use later to illustrate lectures. They were invited, as outstanding experts, far and wide. They were finally among the world's most learned experts on the migratory Monarch butterfly.

Both were involved together in the breeding, feeding and observing. And in the camera work. It was the wife who grew best at telling the tales of the Monarch butterfly, his habits and his habitats, his feeding fancies, his colors and customs and all the other lore—from larvae to winged elegance. Fortunately, she is able to do the total job now since she became a widow.

It seems rather a kindness for this couple to have pleasantly created together this part of her inheritance. Her confident knowledge surely transcends the emotionally empty economics of such an otherwise impersonal annuity. I have no idea of their circumstance but I know that she is busy and happy.

One of the most realistic expectations couples need to face in advance is the fact that at some time during their retirement one of them will probably be left alone. Experience demonstrates that the increased life expectancy of men has still not kept pace with the life expectancy advances also being made by women. So, we end up about where we have always been except that each will have had more years—and they will have had more years in which to share and enjoy their mutual cares and resources, together.

IT PAYS to keep on repeating the question: "What do you expect from your retirement?"

What do you expect to do with all that leisure? All that time in which to accomplish things? It's a question of rust or bust. Would it be better to roar on resolutely toward a happy and explosive life of accomplishment in retirement? Or is it saner to settle comfortably into your "rest and relaxation" rocking chair, keeping time more calmly with other comrades who have already spent their spleen?

You will have plenty of leisure time. The question remains—what are you going to do with it?

Invest it or squander it? Harness it to your hobbies or to your retirement ambitions? Will you let time sift through the fingers of your remaining years—until it is gone—without sufficient reward? Each to his own. It's a free time! Remember? It's your time!

Recreation is a good and necessary ingredient of a balanced life, whether one is working or retired. But recreation means more than just playtime. It offers time to re-create. It provides for changes which bring new interests to new ideas, to give us new verve. To increase our sense of wellbeing. To enjoy the excitement of new involvement.

Not that resting is all bad. It is vital to most of us. But rest alone can lead to rust—dull and boring emptiness. Extra rest is necessary if one is not well enough to keep ripping around. If one has a health requirement for extra sleep and extra care. On the other hand, if one is energetic, determined and involved, it's okay to feed these appetites realistically. It is important to be able to tell the difference. Not just what "they" say we need—but what we feel we need. Try things. Try action. Try nothing. Settle for what pleases your situation.

The trick is to work out individually how much horsepower each of us is willing to hitch to his rocking chair. Whether to point it North into the wild blue yonder of fishing and hunting? Whether to steer it Southward for sun and fun; Toward the East or West, whichever pleases you and the Missus best?

We may not be kids anymore when we retire.

But we shouldn't be expected to subdue all of the joys of our approaching bonus childhood attuned more to the restrained and restricted living habits which seem appropriate for the elderly.

Who says we are elderly? Not quite yet. Perhaps you will want to rocket off in your rocking chair, in all directions at the same time, to find out how much of life's remaining nectar you can still gather and savor. Maybe now is the time for you to go out there to help solve some of your neighbor's nagging problems. Why not bring some action and some answers into the worrisome circumstances of a wide segment of that neglected brotherhood we keep calling the human race.

Motorize your rocking chair—for awhile—in advance. Test retirement as you would test with your toes the cool waters of an unfamiliar lake. Taste and sample to determine how much or how little involvement is best for you. You are not starting over at the beginning. You are starting past the middle—preparing to work toward an end. There are probably realities that are sensible. Realities about what our expectations finally ought to be.

Expectations can cheat people badly but people more often short-change themselves!

A women we knew years ago was a refugee from an angry European time. Her greatest disillusionment was not so much in leaving everything behind which had been near and dear to her family. Except perhaps her grand piano. She was exceedingly disappointed that the promised land she had adopted, along with her husband and family, had streets made of bricks, and gravel and sand and cement. Nowhere were there streets paved with anticipated gold. However much they were impressed by the size and scope of new cities and their adopted country, she did not easily forget her disappointment.

Who can say that it was only she who was wrong? Not that the gold wasn't there—but that her expectation was not more flexible and realistic. Severe disappointments can be avoided by setting more sensible sights. By testing those you can. By responding with resilience to what you find when you get there—anywhere.

Most of us have enjoyed our lives—give or take a few of the extreme surprises. Most of us have not lived lives of round-the-world cruises every year or two. Most are not accustomed to caviar and champagne at every Sunday's brunch. Why should we be surprised if the Sundays of our retirement lack these things? Most of us have not been able, because of time and circumstance, to develop professional level skills in golfing, or painting, in getting very rich or in enhancing our natural beauty and appeals as the years have worn on. Why, then, should we sit disconsolately on new found beaches, moaning away the mornings and afternoons, remeasuring our lousy luck at not finding our own "streets of gold?"

REHEARSE BEFORE YOU RETIRE

Try to avoid having to repeat a bad job of retirement preparation.

Keep on dreaming! Keep trying to capture those beckoning butterflies of new experiences. To cry out when we cannot capture all of them is simply too childish. Too arrogant and too immature an expectation.

Though we often fear otherwise, most of us will have about enough money to get us comfortably through the fading-appetite-period of our retirement. Most of us will probably leave just about enough of an estate for our kids and other relatives to (a) be disappointed that it isn't more and (b) quarrel about how it should be spent.

We are reminded of a wonderful lady who had taught school for several generations and by devotion to her tasks and her charges had been able to save a decent part of what she had earned. She was closeted with her attorney, getting her house in order just before her retirement. He was making out her will. Having established her family relationships and drawn a record of her resources together, the attorney asked what her principal heir, a niece, would probably do when she eventually received her aunt's inheritance.

"I suppose Nancy will take a trip around the world when she finally gets what's left of my money."

The attorney smiled and looked out of the

window, wondering wistfully. His client interrupted him with a surprising suggestion.

"You know, I think I'll take that trip myself. Help me plan for it right now. Help me arrange everything so that I can go and enjoy that experience myself."

Lucky lady! Why shouldn't she go? Why should we be concerned with what others might like to do—after we're gone? Why should you and I concern ourselves—except where obvious needs and responsibilities exist—with what those who remain behind will do with what we have left after we are gone? Why not live it up a little to put some added frosting on the cake of life? To push out further our still expanding horizons. To enrich our remaining years with new meaning, new purpose and new insights. To give us understanding and joy—and new things to think about, to become involved in.

Not everyone has all that much money. Not everyone has that much of a problem.

But each of us has something. An unsatisfied ambition to try something new. An unanswered challenge to repay by sharing with someone else some of what we have learned or gathered as we passed through our working life. To be shared with the new generation that is coming right behind us.

It is a human responsibility, as in conservation forestry, to "replant a tree where one is cut down"—to replace and re-create in someone else that good which we have taken or benefited from.

REHEARSE BEFORE YOU RETIRE

How many there were who have helped us? We ought to do something responsible with the good we have gained, which we could now enjoy sharing with others.

Expectations should be sensible and attainable. Different for different people.

It is possible that you might retire without having rehearsed for your retirement. It is also possible for you to quit without having something to move on *to*. What is simply being stressed here is that it has been found that it works out better if we have a goal, an objective and a plan. To have practiced to assure that the plan will work.

What really matters most to any retiring family is the personal determination that you will expect to enjoy what you find in retirement or that you will try to find what you can enjoy. Platitudes perhaps. But, without a purposeful resolve to get started right you may arrive in your promised land empty-handed and be easily disappointed. It is not necessary to be disappointed—to miss being ready.

Examine the sentiment of one of the broadcast philosophers whose message I caught one day on a car radio. He suggested that we consider the idea of going to the Mediterranean seacoast—to sit for a full year facing the sea, thinking new thoughts, charting a new life.

I haven't the slightest idea what would come into one's head on day number one, in week number five or in month number ten, but it is a disturbing and challenging idea. The promise of this theory seems to be that, having sat there, thinking and meditating on one's life, will so much change who we are and what we do that we would never again during the rest of our lives be the same. I dare say it may be true. For one thing, we'd probably be terribly sunburned—if not sunstruck. Or we might turn into beach bums. It's possible one might become a new kind of instant sage—returning with answers for many of the world's questions. I'm not sure that answers to hunger and want and the need for basic security for much of the human race will be found on exotic blue beaches or on any other beaches.

But who can say that a better way to feed our exploding multitudes might not grow out of the fertile thinking time of such a quiet blue circumstance?

It is often said in creative process teaching that it isn't so much the size of the page or the cost of research in depth but it is rather the size of the idea. Who knows with any certainty what Einstein was thinking about when he discovered the theory that resolved relativity questions? Why was Newton under that apple tree exactly when gravity bumped him on the head?

Who says you have to be at a desk, at a machine or on a farm to figure out how corn, wheat, soybeans—or a new kind of world-wide rice production, or things you can grow in the sea can be grown, harvested and distributed better? Who can say that it

REHEARSE BEFORE YOU RETIRE

can't be thought—by you—on the seacoasts of Spain, in Florida, at a lake in Vermont or in a park in Paducah?

One word of high warning. Don't set goals and expectations beyond your normal and comfortable experience. Avoid the unrealistically unattainable. Why seek guaranteed disappointment? Set your sights near the end of your reach—far enough so that you can almost touch them.

If you want an important challenge, think of this conflict of circumstance: two kinds of explosions exist in the world. One is the people explosion almost everywhere and the other is the simultaneous explosion of new and unimagined degrees of worldly affluence—but which is not being enjoyed by everyone, or everywhere.

Sit on your own "Spanish seacoast" right where you are right now. Dream practically for a while about all the things all of those people will need, all of the services they will demand, all of the things they can already buy and may further hope to want.

Imagine what can be done for them to help them attain less uneven lives and happier circumstances.

The mind reels at the task. Think of all that needs doing, all that remains to be done. If you will only grab onto your own brass ring—to swing sensibly but creatively—onto your own stage, ready to play your best role with realistic but promising retirement expectations. Be confident about what you expect because you have rehearsed for the goals you will retire *to*.

ACTION IDEAS TO THINK ABOUT:

How Will You Respond to Retirement—Once You're There?

	Yes	No
Will you be satisfied with life?	—	—
Will you be comfortable?	—	—
Do you expect to get interested in new people and things?	—	—
Are you generally grateful for having had good health; a good life?	—	—
Do you expect to get involved again?	—	—
How do you expect you will be at accepting the retirement you find?	—	—
Are you going to be a full time worrier and complainer?	—	—
Will you do something to help make it work better—beforehand?	—	—

4

Inventory Your Retirement Resources

ANY discussion on preparation for retirement presupposes that you still have that option—to prepare. This subject might, however, also concern an already retired person. Therefore, this specific section fits either.

Of all the resources you and I must try to bring into retirement to make it as successful as possible, none is more absolutely vital than what is implied in this all too obvious warning:

> "The Single Most Important Thing You Must Save For Your Retirement *is Yourself."*

Probably the second most important item on the retirement resources agenda might be that of bringing along a loyal and understanding mate. Ac-

How Long Will You Need Retirement Income?

Check these life expectancy tables—for averages,

AGE	MALE	FEMALE	AVERAGE/TOTAL
50	23	28	26
55	19	24	22
60	16	20	18
62	15	19	17
65	13	16	15

That's how long you will need retirement income.

Figures like these reflect experience; and the average of populations. Family histories; longevity; genes; all those other contributing factors. So is the loving care you give yourself . . . and avoiding bad luck; accidents.

The difference between what you own and what you owe is the net worth picture you live with. But you can't live on net worth—not really. What regular, monthly and annual, income will your net assets produce?

*_____

Do you have a clear picture of how to determine how much income you will need; for how long; how it's coming to you—and from what asset sources?

*_____

How much would it help your attitude toward retirement if you understood how much income you could count on regularly—once your paycheck stops?

*_____

Will you now determine your money needs and income expectations?

*_____

REHEARSE BEFORE YOU RETIRE

tually, these two points are interrelated. Some women's husbands don't make it to retirement. These ladies arrive at their "promised land"—alone. In some cases there may have been steps the two of them might have taken to help both reach retirement—together.

When we count resources we usually think of money, property, talent and know-how. None of these will be worth much to you if you do not also have reasonably good health. Good health (and not necessarily perfect health) is a most vital resource. It concerns both men and women. Annual physical check-ups are an intelligent practice. They give doctors the opportunity to spot developing problems before they progress too far. Listening to one's doctor makes plain good sense.

Most men abuse themselves in too many ways. Life does not make it easy for us to live moderately. We overwork and overworry. We overeat and overdrink. We undersleep and under-vacation. We run around with less confidence in the cosmos and less faith in God than we ought to have. We do a terrible job—racing through life without taking the time to develop a comforting philosophy of life. Most of us do substantial harm to ourselves by carrying the heavy burden of worried looks on our face and a worried slouch on our shoulders. We forget to walk away from our troubles—head held high, unconcerned.

If physical health is important for the employed, to keep them working, it is doubly important for those who are retiring. I can't imagine less fun than to be feeling poorly and not working at the same time. With all that time to think about all that trouble. Try to bring along a happy attitude—along with your health.

Wives can help their husbands moderate—not so much by nagging as by scheduling time off—for long vacations and long weekends. By setting more interesting tables loaded more with delightful tastes and attractive servings and less with sheer tonnage. By suggesting fruit instead of frappes. By skimping on helpings and increasing the ceremony. By sitting down at table before—not after—too many *extra* before dinner cocktails.

By helping the old boy, against his weak-kneed will, to moderate. By cutting down on late midweek hours, by minimizing midweek involvements. By arranging and policing nap times and sleep time for both of you. And by continuing or beginning to exercise—with him. Exercise is probably not bad for women. It's absolutely essential for today's hard-working, hard-driving, hard-eating and drinking, and hardheaded American male.

While we're concerning ourselves with resources, it's easy to forget about saving ourselves—and our good health. These are the "without-which-not" of successful retirement. For without them, there will be a somewhat less carefree retirement.

REHEARSE BEFORE YOU RETIRE

And if you don't both arrive there alive, you won't be having a happy and married retirement either.

On to other resources. There are five principal resource questions every man must ask and every wife must help him answer as satisfactorily as is appropriate to individual circumstances. Questions like these:

A. How much retirement *money* will you have—to spend?

B. How's your retirement *health*—really?

C. How much of a *drag* will your "companion" be—in retirement?

D. What are you most *afraid* of—about being retired?

E. What *boredom* quotient are you bringing into retirement?

Let's take them one at a time.

Depending upon which pre-retirement year you are in, or what your financial lot in life may have been, or on your own level of prudence and foresight, you either have saved, are saving or intend to save necessary and helpful dollar resources for your retirement.

Money has power. It can help us do more things. Go more places. Enjoy life more. Naturally this also depends on the state of your health and well-being.

But money is not easy to save. Not all by yourself in any event.

If you are hoping and planning to retire at 62, as just one example, Social Security will pay you and your wife up to 80 percent of the amount you would collect if you waited to begin receiving such payments at age 65. The difference in doing it one way rather than the other has been calculated. If you begin collecting Social Security at age 62, you receive more benefits earlier. It would otherwise take you from 12 to 15 extra years to make up for what you would have missed by *not* taking it then.

If you are otherwise able and are interested in retiring at 62 this may be best for you. Some should wait until 65—and some will need to. Others will never want to quit. In any case, retirement income factors like these will probably moderate still further especially if retirement practices move the earlier quitting age to 60.

Most men will also be receiving some kind of pension—either from company pension funds, from retirement trust plans where they work or from self-employed tax relief programs which are possible now. Plans like these keep changing from year to year but they usually do not diminish. If anything, they will increase in what they provide even though inflation will probably continue to nibble away at the final result.

The major point to be made here is that additional income from retirement pension programs is a fact which can be investigated where you work. It can become a fact if you seek the counsel of

REHEARSE BEFORE YOU RETIRE 123

attorneys, insurance and banking people who specialize in advising on these new programs. Specific examples are too varied to set down here. What is not so difficult to establish, however, is your own net worth.

COMPLETE YOUR OWN NET WORTH CHART
(next two pages)

WHEN it comes to lining up resources for retirement, no experience story matches that of my friend, Jackie Halterman. I believe Jackie enlisted in the Navy at about 17 or 18. He progressed in his ratings and eventually moved up into the officer ranks. He had a hobby of photography and the bug kept him happily and successfully busy. This led him into a specialty in the personnel bureau of the Navy where eventually he was put in charge of film-making and photographic duties for the recruiting service.

He had also gone the full route of full-fledged seaman and Naval officer in charge of ships and stations. Since Jackie saw risky duty, he sometimes got extra pay. The pay he received was more than he then needed.

He didn't so much save it. But he did begin investing in one of the early-day mutual fund programs. He bought securities systematically, even though his early purchases were not large. In time, the profits and progress he made became known to some of his shipmates and he was asked to help them

WHAT WE OWN

Assets Right Now   At Retirement

Money

	Right Now	At Retirement
Cash on hand	$ _____	$ _____
Checking Accounts	_____	_____
Savings Accounts	_____	_____
Government Bonds (accrued value)	_____	_____
Common or Preferred Stocks (market value)	_____	_____
Other Bonds (market value)	_____	_____
*Life Insurance (cash values)	_____	_____
Real Estate (our home)	_____	_____
Other Real Estate (appraised values)	_____	_____
Automobiles (market values)	_____	_____
Personal Property (household and other)	_____	_____
Notes You Hold (any money due you)	_____	_____
Pensions	_____	_____
Retirement Trust Funds (profit-sharing)	_____	_____
Stock Options (any deferred income)	_____	_____
Regular Dividends and Interest (expected)	_____	_____
Social Security Payments (secure estimate)	_____	_____
Government, Service Disability Payments	_____	_____
Any Other (rents, royalties, etc.)	_____	_____
TOTAL ASSETS (What We Own)	$ _____	$ _____

* Life Insurance: You may wish to figure principal amounts (death values) at now amounts for now column, and cash values for the retirement column.

WHAT WE OWE

Liabilities   Right Now   At Retirement

Money

Current Bills .... $ _____ $ _____
Contributions (committed or ongoing) .. _____ _____

Installment Debt (balances)

Mortgage on Home .... _____ _____
Mortgage on Investment Property ..... _____ _____
Repayment Due on Life Insurance ..... _____ _____
Automobile Loan Payments Due .... _____ _____
Furniture or Appliance Payments ...... _____ _____
Personal Loans .... _____ _____
Doctor and Hospital (balances) .... _____ _____
Support (expected by family members) .. _____ _____
Any Other Payments Due .... _____ _____
Balances Due on Stocks or Bonds .... _____ _____
Payments on Life Insurance (still due) .... _____ _____
TOTAL LIABILITIES (What We Owe) ...... $ _____ $ _____

WHAT WE OWN (Assets) .... $ _____ $ _____
WHAT WE OWE (Liabilities) .... $ _____ $ _____
TOTAL NET WORTH (The Difference) ... $ _____ $ _____

begin investment programs. He was able to help them by becoming an unofficial representative of the type of mutual fund that had been serving him.

The money tree grew. For Jackie and for many of his shipmates. After he was in the Navy 20 years he retired and moved to sunny southern Florida. Lots of servicemen seem to retire there. He kept right on representing his mutual fund, selling securities and savings programs to old shipmates, to their friends and to new neighbors and new friends. Now he has several men who work for him throughout his section of the state.

He also still keeps his hand in filming and photography. He signs on occasionally as a crew member with a TV filming group on special assignments. This film job is more for love than for the money. But it also enables him to play golf whenever they go to shoot on movie locations. Jackie plays golf most days and has become quite good at it. He also travels—as much as two months of the year, to far away and interesting places which his time in the Navy brought to his attention and which time in early retirement now offers him for a fuller time for enjoyment.

Jackie planned for his retirement by preparing to retire *to* something and by having rehearsed for it endlessly. He established exceedingly sensible expectations because he knew exactly what he would be doing and what kind of cash flow income he would be enjoying. He saved his health and brought it with him into an early retirement. He also saved enough of the dollars and some of the good sense of his Navy time to guarantee freedom and comfort for himself and his family in retirement—to a new life, a good and full life. That's what he keeps telling me.

Not all of us can go all the way back—to do over the things we didn't get started at early enough in order to live like Jackie. But most of us can still do quite a bit from age 45, or 50, or 55, to get our houses in better order so that we will have sufficient auxiliary dollars to augment Social Security and the pension most of us are now reasonably assured of.

Chances are, most of us will have slightly more money available for our retirement than we will have appetites and energy left to enjoy these resources.

There are people today—and there will probably always be—who have a hard time making ends meet in retirement because of their fixed circumstances which have not kept pace with continuing inflation. But if a man saves his health, he can usually find some work to keep him busy part-time in retirement. Work that matches his interests, his health and ability—and which will bring some new money to add to retirement's dwindling pile.

WHAT about your health? You and I can't do much any more to make it better. But you have your doctor and he probably does quite well to keep it from getting worse—to keep it as good as it is. We have to expect a certain amount of what doctors knowingly refer to as the aging process. We can't jump quite as high—or as often. We don't even want to run quite as fast or as far as formerly. We have probably discovered by now that we can't eat all the cake the world can bake or drink all the spirits it can distill or ferment. The beginning of wisdom is in that knowledge. There will always be enough of it to please our palates. It's a necessity and fair play besides for us to leave a little for tomorrow and for the other guy. Taste and savor each sip of the fruits of life. Enjoy them more lovingly—and less gluttonously.

There are pills to make you happy, to keep you happy, to help you sleep, to keep you awake. There are potions to protect against sudden changes in individual health patterns. There are warnings about alcohol and the liver. About smoking and the lungs. About high speed driving and high speed dying. Not all of us listen to all we should hear. And yet most of us also fuss too much about our health. It's a self-centered hobby which exacts its own price. Worrying about one's health can scarcely make it better and certainly makes us less fun to be with. Sensible concern is all that most of us are expected to exercise. So that we will remember to be moderate—to enjoy and to live.

Half the rest of your health problem is in the hands of your doctor. If he isn't a good enough doctor in your opinion, find one in whom you can place your faith. Trust and pay him to keep you well as the Chinese do. Forget about yourself. It costs money to be sick and you can use such money better to enjoy your retirement. Hope to be well. Enjoy life in good health. It's your first and last wealth.

There are so many more facts which might be reviewed about the significance of wealth and health and about their contribution to a more satisfactory retirement life. We do not think it necessary for this planning process since they are essential facts with which all of you are familiar. It is well to remind you to arrive at your retirement time with all of your assets reasonably intact.

Retirement resources include Social Security, pension funds, annuities, other insurance programs, savings, property and securities. Or they may come as new income from some new activity which might grow out of a skill, a hobby or a small business you might decide to try. It's important to recognize that money makes some difference. It's also important to face the fact that a lot of money won't make a lot of difference—for most of us.

Caution about health and health attitudes should not suggest that one begin systematic programs of concern and worry. Rather, it seems sensible for most of us to keep our wits about us, to bring along a happy attitude, to be willing to simplify our living, to have things that are compelling for us to do. To have an agenda of ideas and thoughts we want to think about and develop. Good things we want to share. A tranquil heart and an even temper ready to enjoy living the remainder of life. Beyond such practical preparations, we should probably joyfully accept each day with its rain and shine variations. With its up and down scales, its pro and con results. Whoever said we always were going to enjoy only an even and monotonous pleasantness. We can learn to appreciate what comes our way by learning about the other things and the other circumstances we would care even less for.

It seems unnecessary to suggest that people approaching retirement have business affairs to look after. Business for a trusted attorney, for the trust department of their bank, for their insurance agent, for social security offices, for real estate advisors and for a lot of other fiscal people. It follows that they also have need for getting and keeping their health household in order. We must assume that's part of a family's housekeeping as retirement time approaches. So that you will have done all you can to protect all you have. So that you can stop thinking about it.

High on your list of any inventory of retirement resources you must include the mate you are bringing with you. Any man needs to think about the kind of husband he has been, the kind he must be to help make the new life in retirement work. Wives don't need more of a husband. Most have had just about enough of him by this time. But they do need us and they admit it. Not many of them yearn

REHEARSE BEFORE YOU RETIRE 131

to be widows. So hang onto your health and sharpen up your attitudes about what kind of retired guy you will be. Day-after-day and year-after-year.

Honestly now. What about the Missus? How much of a drag is your wife apt to be? Blessed are you if she is simply cheerful, charming, lovely. A happy companion. Many are. A few are not.

Wives generally dread changed routines which bring an interrupted flow in the habits and security of life. Many wives have worked and helped build the family's security and retirement resources. Today many women have highly developed skills— talents which it would be a shame to deny to their world. It might also be wrong to deny them the satisfactions of such doing and contributing.

Some wives are not going to be ready for retirement. Or even for the task of planning for retirement. These are the girls we have to talk to. Face it ladies. Face the facts of retirement. Finding your husband without a job, without an income. Might as well face these facts because they will be facing you before long. Facts are foolish to hide from. It doesn't do much good to say you can't bear to think of it, that it depresses you, that your husband is not ready to start quitting. To give up. He isn't an old man.

All of these thoughts may be true. But the fact remains that you can't hide your ostrich head from all of the problems you imagine you will find in retirement. You may have less joy in retirement if you lack the willingness to help face it now.

Join in the fun of fixing up your "new life raft" now so that you can float down the remaining years of your lives—happily toward some serene harbor where your rehearsing has indicated you will be most content.

Accept the fact that each new day will not be like each old day of years past. Thank your lucky stars that this is true. Welcome new days and seek new ways. Draw heavily upon your good sense, lady. Be glad that you possess sensible expectations. If you are the type who joyfully accepts her lot in life, who changes what she can change, and who accepts that which can't be changed, you are fortunate. You will be a great asset and an important resource for the happy retirement for your tired-out "paymate." He may not be tired out and he may not be old. But he will be even less so if you are not a retirement drag. It costs no more for you to smile. To join in the fun. You helped him early—to make a good life for you and the family—by sacrificing, by learning to do for yourselves, by taking each day as it came.

Why not begin again to be the kind of bride that made it all work in the first place?

Both of you must now remember that life is really a parade of little things. Little events which are punctuated periodically by occasionally bigger problems. Happiness in retirement, like happiness in any time of life, is not so much in having all that will

REHEARSE BEFORE YOU RETIRE

make us happy. It is rather how we respond, how happily we accept that which we do have. To share and to enjoy.

There's a formula-for-happiness story I like that makes a poignant point. It involves old friends who had marital, money and mental problems—all mixed together. One or the other was usually either seeking financial advice, physical advice, temperance advice—or mental health help. It was a strain on the family and a drain on their resources. They struggled grimly, unhappily onward.

After a number of years of lost contact, word came from these old acquaintances. We inquired about her health, his more sobered welfare and their life's present bugaboos. The husband had a sad but winsome tale to tell. He admitted that his wife still had psychological problems which required the regular help of a psychiatrist. But she was working now as receptionist and secretary to her psychiatrist—earning her own payments for these services.

The money alone wasn't the only payment—or the only important ingredient of her progress.

Now, he reported, when this bothered "bride" came home for family dinner, she sat down to recite—not her depressions, fears, troubles and concerns. Instead, she brought news about the problems and progress of other unnamed patients who visited her doctor-employer. She was able to tell these tales with sympathetic understanding, without personal involvement or self-pitying sadness.

This true life story indicates well how, in a new and sensible way, one family solved its togetherness problems—problems which had originally threatened to drive them all into sadder and separate lives.

As you take your inventory of resources, find out what you are most concerned about as you approach retirement. Since we have examined the problem of dollars, health and well being, and the attitudes of your good wife—what's left? Are you afraid of living too long or dying too soon? Are you worried that you might not make it to retirement? Are you unsure where you will go, what you will do, what it will be like when you retire?

If we are being reasonably temperate, keeping body and soul soundly together, we are probably managing our health and welfare program about as well as we can. The rest really ought to be in the hands of the doctors and their systems. They get paid for knowing how to help us. At today's rates we must also assume part of the pay goes to cover the concern they hold about us.

Even for those who worry without an agenda, there are exercises and programs to pursue.

It would probably help you to write down the things that you are most concerned about. Talk them over with your wife and check off those which she can handle. It will give her something to do and involve her in your program. Take the rest to your clergyman, to your doctor or your lawyer—and let

REHEARSE BEFORE YOU RETIRE

these professionals dispose of these problems. Your list is getting smaller.

Now set down any remaining fears, doubts or concerns and find an expert who can help you with them. Attack a few yourself so that you don't run out of preparation duties. When your list is done and you've had your fun worrying about it, assume that you have checked off everything. You're done with that job. Throw your list away and forget that you had unsolved concerns.

On to the next question.

It's a good idea for each of us to measure our appetite for, or inclination to, boredom. People vary in their adaptability to new circumstances, new surroundings, new neighborhoods and a new way of living. Not everyone knows, or has the psychic resources, to get involved in new ideas, new projects, new work or new opportunities for enriching life.

Try it!

It may seem strange to those of us who never have time for all the things we want to do, to see and learn about, to find that there are people who don't know where to begin. This is an important fact about people's personal resources which we must recognize. Neither money nor position can alter these facts of life for the people who find time hanging heavy on their hands. It seems unnecessary to be bored. The world is full of libraries, museums, shops, stores and services for anyone who wants to learn a skill. To learn or practice for something new—or even to make a little money selling your skills. But there may be some among us who do not possess personal motivation or the psychological resourcefulness to begin to reach out—to make an advantage of their assets.

Boredom, confusion and personal drift are a fact of some people's lives. Some weary of the task at hand more quickly than others. Others are annoyed when time runs out. They never seem able to get everything done. Your psychological resources for retirement are as important for the success of your golden years as any other ingredient. Within families, either the husband or the wife may be the one who possesses the drive to enrich life. This can help, or harass, depending upon the psychological sensitivity of the more active partner.

Those who are easily bored would do well to make specific plans. Include details about times, places and things to do, things to see and people to meet. Without such a plan they could drift from nothing to nowhere and loathe the leisure that has made it all so abundantly possible. Treat leisure as a perishable gift.

We have in mind a true senior citizen, mother of a friend of ours. She finally and reluctantly retired to what she called her old people's home. They have slicker names today but these are homes for people who are not incapacitated. Activities abound and a wide variety of participation is brought to bear on the task of filling time.

REHEARSE BEFORE YOU RETIRE 137

Our lady was reluctant to leave "her home"—even to visit her son and daughter-in-law for Thanksgiving dinner—because of all the activities, excitement and personal relationships she might be missing out on at "the home." This lady was never lacking in resources. She knew how to do many things and she wished to do many more. She had one of the area's most outstanding, interesting and varied button collections.

You and I may frown a bit about making a fuss over buttons but bless her happy heart. Our Mrs. Kaye filled her mind and life with the lore of everything involving buttons; she had buttons to spare and buttons from everywhere. She knew her buttons—about many things.

That isn't all about Mrs. Kaye. She took to doing color retouching of the color print reproduction process and from this, past age 80, she developed into an amateur portraitist. Had she lived even longer than her 85 years, our friend might have turned out to be something even more special. She had always been special—with wide new interests which led to more newly developed talents. She welcomed more new curiosities than she and her busy days and years could ever get around to. Such a person wouldn't understand boredom problems. She understood the personal resources people need to bring with them into retirement. All of us can acquire more. We need to give thought to the task—

before we retire—to increase the certainty that our resource quota will be filled.

It's a good idea when one begins to take it easy, to make a list (husband and wife together if they can agree to do it calmly and uncritically) of individual assets and liabilities as these will relate to the new life they are looking toward in retirement.

Some habits are hidden in the busyness of daily living. Other tendencies may be obscured because we don't have time to have them get in our way. Given extra free time and a lack of regimen which blessed retirement provides, some of these little nuisances could become nagging negatives. Face them on paper cooperatively and candidly. Through friendly and determined collaboration, prepare to minimize those which matter and to agree to ignore those which don't matter very much at all.

"How you hold your cigarette. The way you sniffle or snore. Walk on your heels, look off into space or stare right through me, dear."

Personal idiosyncracies can be annoying even in the busy time of normal living. We have more time to notice—to be upset, once we reach retirement's new free time.

"Perhaps we ought to sweep these out of our mind or hide them under the rug of it-doesn't-really-matter, dear. Go ahead and sniffle! But, please! Don't snore quite so loudly, quite so often!"

There are realities about personal resources that need to be faced before retirement.

REHEARSE BEFORE YOU RETIRE

WE KNOW of several talented people who tried semi-retirement to write. They hoped to write what they self-consciously called the great American novel. One of these folks had a heart attack and decided to save the rest of his life for himself. He quit to write his book. I do not think that he has had the novel published but those other sports-oriented volumes he wrote in collaboration with national sports personalities have led to fat incomes for him and for his associates. They have sold in tens of thousands of volumes because he had the know-how and the business moxie. He knew how to find the sponsors he needed and how to deliver a good project at a profit.

Who cares that his earlier and grander idea of writing fiction didn't take quite the direction he originally had in mind. He did write books, produced them and he did go on living—well. He is still doing great and has enjoyed many happy years of an exciting life which keeps him in touch with many more of his favored sports personalities than his previous work life had ever provided.

He took a different fork in the road and it turned out better than the one he had originally intended. One must keep a light-hearted attitude and be willing to fit one's resources to the pathway one ends up traveling on.

We remember another young man who tried somewhat the same writing direction. But he found himself incapable, or too undisciplined and untalented. The last we heard of him was about that drinking syndrome which often seems to touch the discouraged and unsuccessful ones. Too bad—but success is often such a subjective judgment. It can really nag at our private heart.

Most of us are not all we had hoped to be. But we are what we are. That should be sufficient if we are capable of facing the fact that what we are is apparently what was generally intended for us. The acceptance of our lot in life, the acceptance of how we can still improve that lot should be enough for most. But we often want more—or think the world expects more of us. The world, unfortunately, really doesn't care all that much. It is our response to what we become—or don't become—that is the price we pay in self-respect and in personal peace.

Still another writer; this one a very young man with a wife and child set off for an island in the sun. To write exotic and unreal stories. All we ever heard him tell of that year or two of lost weekends was about sailing from day to day. Flying from landing strip to landing strip, on sortie after sortie—touching down here and there, friend after friend, fickle fancy after fickle fancy, to add still more rum to what had become a really rummy way of life. Without much purpose and without any satisfying result.

Without result, except the necessity to come back to reality. To face the hard fact that he didn't

REHEARSE BEFORE YOU RETIRE 141

happen to be a Hemingway. He couldn't become any real part of being a real Hemingway except that part which was still being served at all the island bars.

The world should not discourage the dreamer or the doer who wishes to try. Lots of people don't know that they can't do things. Their successes are listed high among those others who have accomplished so much in life. Some are unrealistic about their own human and personal resources. Once tried and found wanting beyond reasonable doubt, we should not lose anything more than a touch of our pride if we must come back "to our father" without beating our breast in prodigal penitence forevermore.

The world keeps starting over, its many failures to correct. Even at 50 or 55—or 65—it's a good time to begin over. To add another chapter, to write still another page in the story of our life. Don't be afraid to try—and don't be afraid to admit it if it doesn't work out. Most are better off for the experience of reaching out and trying.

Reality and resources have many faces.

We knew a retired farmer who came to town to live at the community's little hotel. Nothing to do after an extremely active life. This bothered him. He wearied of relative-visiting, of chatting aimlessly in small talk marathons with the other rocking chair veterans. He was troubled also about using up his dollar resources. He feared being sick for a long time without the means to pay. He wanted no part of falling back upon his children. His modest but meaningful answer: a modest job as night clerk at the hotel which housed him—working only every other night. Just enough dollars to keep him almost even. Just enough responsibility and purpose in life to keep up his self-esteem. Just enough activity to keep him from rusting restlessly away. This true tale, among so many more, always seemed the nicest ending for a lifetime of hard-working days. What a calm reality to find that he was able to earn his keep through a little easy effort so close to his bed and board.

People face their preparation problems in interesting ways. One wonders whether they all have these ideas in mind before the fact or whether it occurs to them halfway through their routine.

Another neighbor we know prepares and repairs lawns for people. He trims trees and prunes shrubs out of love for the task. For this he collects extra moonlighting money. It has never been clear whether the business of caring for growing things came first, or whether the recompense was his principal reward.

This fellow has full employment in a factory which produces heavy equipment. He helped establish the accounting department of his company. We know that as his young family grows into a variety of schooling expenses, each progressively takes on tasks and earns income by himself. Many families use this

REHEARSE BEFORE YOU RETIRE 143

way to help each other through life. By listening carefully we have become aware that he does this lawn care avocationally now for extra income because it is needed now. He also intends to do more of the same to provide some of his own retirement resources. It really doesn't matter what lawn and garden motivations move this man. But it does matter that he has something which serves him now, pleases him meanwhile—and which offers his own phasing out, phasing down, for turning to full time at a later time in his life.

If our investigations and our research have shown one thing it is the comforting fact that more and more people are making positive moves toward better living now and for fuller living later than one would readily imagine.

We have other friends who used a three-week vacation to rehearse in one short course for their own retirement. They enrolled in a southern university to begin the process of learning sculpting. They also sat and sunned on the beaches. They attended art shows—and night club shows—and did the other things tourists do. But during the principal time of each day, for three weeks, they were associated with sculptors who taught the wife to work in stone and the man to carve in wood.

His was a special kind of learning because he worked with a chain saw on large logs. His results were monumental in size if not in significance. He calls them grotesque whimsies. These works have been shown in one-man shows and they have sold. The wife may have gone along for the spirit of the idea but we found her stone work every bit as promising as his wood-whittling. There are hidden abilities in most hands and in most hearts. We need to take the time, to make a break and seek out teachers who can help us find these extra values. Such new creative ventures can make all the difference—especially after life slows down and the days get longer with more time for trying more new things. Keep your exploration spirit alive.

One way to solve your resource proposition, to help your inventory look more promising, is to set down what you singularly have to offer. What do you do? What have you ever done? What did you do as a child, as a student, as an early family person? What have you to give to others? Or what can you expect from them in the process of sharing what you know, what you can do, what you can teach?

Each of us is an individual and each must accept this friendly fact. No one would shoe horses exactly like we might do it. Or carve in stone or wood, or paint a picture. Or collect buttons, or write a poem. We might think they do it better. The world judges that—not we.

Seek the advice of teachers on subjects you find most interesting. Take courses. Take inventory of your present level of skill in things. Perhaps you might teach in the technical and vocational schools which are blossoming across the land. In night schools for young and old—to help those who know little to acquire some of the know-how you have always taken for granted and dismissed as being unimportant. Stop selling yourself short. Sell your interests and re-engage yourself as your own kind of expert.

If you really lack sufficient personal skills and know-how in the tasks and things you would most like to do, begin to build up these skills, this know-how. Do it now. It will help you fill present days and help you build a rousing reservoir to draw upon once you have more time—once you have the psychological need for filling that time.

None of these suggestions strike much of a difference between the retiring husband's prospects and those of the retiring wife. Personal resources don't always have to do with earning a living, with where you live. But they may have a great deal to do with what you will do there. Both of you will have more free time—and fuller lives—if you set your retirement days up right. Both of you will have need for an agenda that's exciting and satisfying to you. One that returns a profit in some king of coin—be it negotiable or psychological.

Take steps now to fill voids and to lengthen lists of what you want to do and what you will be able to do. Build on present strengths, on present and past interests. You will enjoy the process now and be comforted in looking ahead to know that wherever you go you will have more to do than days in which to get it done.

Remember Grandma Moses. She took up painting in her seventies and had to cut paintings in half in order to help meet the demand which mushroomed quickly in the fading remainder of her long and happy life. She, too, found that even a good long life is too short, too quick, with too much of it still unpainted.

People who succeed in business decide in advance on the preparation necessary for success. They read up on the subject. They visit others in the same kind of business. They take courses—including full college courses. They experiment in small ways. Most of those who are successful in business have built upon some talent, skill or experience which is theirs in a special way. This helps guarantee success.

People who are preparing for the approach of retirement are going into a new business, too. It's a business with less income, less chance to sell out and move on to something else. It's a business for which we have had little experience. But it is also an occupation which puts lessened demands upon us. And yet, it is an activity that can be measurably more successful if we will face the facts in advance and prepare well for its coming.

It's sad to hear a retired college dean who was invited back to reminisce with his "boys" at their 25th class reunion lament that he misses those good old days greatly. That he wishes he could once

REHEARSE BEFORE YOU RETIRE

again be their school's dean. That he and Mrs. Dean have so little to do. So few people to see who have time to see them. So little compelling purpose left in life.

It's easy for us to say this educator missed his chance back there somewhere to educate himself for this time of life. It's easy to say it because it is true. But an educator probably has no greater guarantee against such mistakes than those who are less learned. One must prepare and practice. With purpose and goals—one must gather his best resources and add some new ones to his larder for later years.

Some people go at this task gradually. By retiring partially, by tapering off. This is good for some, for practical reasons, bad for others for psychological reasons. It's an option that is not available to everyone by the very nature of one's job, financial or family circumstance. It isn't a bad idea to take such a trip, tentatively—if one is so inclined—especially if you are moving into retirement a little earlier than may be customary.

Those who go toward retirement voluntarily are apt to welcome it more.

This fact is based on the experiences of many. Those who are forced to retire reluctantly are more apt to resist its abruptness and the inevitable doom-like ending. These latter are inclined to have a lost feeling which they lean on, whimpering about almost everything about retirement. They were not ready for it.

Who kept them from thinking ahead?

It has been medically reported that willing retirees show a slower decline in their health during aging years than those who reluctantly accept the hard fact of being finished. Retirement shock must indicate an absence of an adequate resource inventory. An earlier resource hoarding might have filled some of the vacuum.

Do you still lack a clear appreciation of the resources you will need—compared to the resources you have? Perhaps we have been looking at this question too narrowly. Perhaps instead of counting dollars, measuring attitudes and appraising ambitions—instead of worrying about health and wifely points of view, we should have been measuring what needs doing in the world with which you can help.

Let's take a look at just one man's experience and just one stupendous area of opportunity for a lot of retired people who are sorely needed in many ways and in many degrees of involvement.

We know a young missionary who pleaded with his superiors to send him to the Dominican Republic. He had never been there before and had no special reason for wanting to be in that particular place except the sincere wish to find more urgent ways to help neglected souls find a higher level of peace and a little of the progress which had passed them by.

He came back recently on one of his "gathering junkets" after several years of living among his

REHEARSE BEFORE YOU RETIRE

particular congregation of 16,000 Dominican natives.

He smiles from the heart when he talks about his daily duties, about the needs for simple things which we take blithely for granted. He really smiles all over when he tells how much he wishes for us to see his wonderful people. To know their simple lives, their happy hearts, their perilous poverty.

How does that concern you and me?

This young man of God gives us a variety of answers. He needs visitors who will come prepared to help for a time. To bring love and simple learning. To bring basic tools—typewriters and trumpets—buttons and thread. To help make post holes for fence rows around the simplest gardens. To come with so much more helpfulness. Help with older people, healthful help, loving help—the combing of hair, the just being there. Help with little people. To teach simple things. To teach them to pray and play. To work and to learn. To see and hear the world's old and new ideas. To share music and art from other cultures.

Basically what our cleric needs badly is for someone to take his place just a little, during his absences as he rides off on horseback to help prepare a sick parishioner 40 miles away to meet his maker. To remain behind to fill so many and such varied human voids which this one young man of energy sees but cannot solve all by himself.

It is not for us to understand fully how his

people could be helped best except to recognize that the good reverend knows what is needed. He knows what kind of people could help and which kinds would be no good at all. Language would be an inconvenience but that can be surmounted by any who wish to try. Customs of the Dominican culture would be startling to some—merely interesting to others. Obviously, not everyone should take on this kind of do-good thing.

It is sufficient for this report to serve as a specific example of just one area in this needy world where human love and understanding, where practical helpfulness is so urgently needed and so unbelievably successful as it helps overcome a part of the misery and some of the hopelessness which so many of the world's people live with forevermore.

Not every retiring couple can be expected to be suited to such extreme change in life and not everyone needs to go to far away Africa, or Asia or to this Dominican Island. There is within our own country, and within our own community, much that is similar in need.

The United Nations knows where you can help. The World Council of Churches and all of its affiliated denominations and their institutions know. Our own governmental agencies with their people-aid programs know. Write, study, ask and use travel to find out. Find out where you are most needed or where your particular kind of helpfulness would fit best.

REHEARSE BEFORE YOU RETIRE

Ask our young priestly person, or the thousands like him who go out from our shores, what they need most. Perhaps it isn't you and the Missus. Perhaps it isn't people so much as it is the actual establishment and equipping of a new general store. This happens to be an actual accomplishment resulting from a specific gift in answer to a specific need the Reverend indicated to one volunteer.

Another time it was the need for a dozen musical instruments—used or new. The donor asked who was going to teach these people to play all these varied instruments. Our missionary replied that his people are full of music. They will know how to play after being shown simple basics. Send me a typewriter or two. An adding machine for the mission office. Several dozen sewing machines. One organization learned that the most needed thing in one part of India was basic instruction on how to use existing paper supplies there along with other existing materials to manufacture an Indian flypaper—to begin the forbidding process of trapping at least a few of the endless parade of buzzing, stinging and disease-spreading flies.

Use your own imagination. Harness your own interests. Learn about the extremely basic things which are not local to these places where multitudes live out their poor lives. We throw away without thought. We hold garage rummage sales in which we dispose of our third set of dinnerware. We discard utensils, backyard grills, garden cultivators no longer used. We junk still serviceable lawn mowers because we've taken to riding powered monsters. Safety pins, sewing needles, spools upon spools of nylon thread. Or safety razors. You name your own list. The world—near and far—needs us, badly.

WE'VE wandered off idealistically into an inventory of everyday affairs. How do these relate to our own retirement resource inventory?

Finding out what we have, what we want to do with it in our remaining years, is a good place to start. Finding out what our world needs which we could help supply is an excellent added step to take. The world and its people are increasingly our neighbors because of the speed and ease of communications and the speed of moving back and forth.

It isn't just that it's easier for us to get there and to bring help there. We must recognize that it is also easier for all those neglected millions upon millions to learn and yearn for what we have. They see how much we waste, and they hope, perhaps for the first time and for the first generation in their land to dare to expect to have similar benefits—to share in the life-giving and life-prolonging uses of just a little of what we casually cast aside.

Speak to the people who go out to our own poor—our own frontiers—whether it be in our ghettos or on our mountains. Speak to the folks who travel to far-off underprivileged and underdeveloped regions. Search out returning peace corps volunteers

REHEARSE BEFORE YOU RETIRE

and seek to zero-in on the life and times of the places these young people have seen and served.

Use your experienced imagination constructively and positively. Find in your own inventory of your own personal resources a small part of the answer for meeting some of the needs of just a few of those who do without, of those who are trying to help them do just a little better.

Wouldn't you really like for part of the remainder of your life to be giving back to your world rather than to remain obsessed with still more getting for yourselves?

Perhaps there is no greater resource in us as members of our human society than that which recognizes that our lot is good and that our inventory is large. So huge, in fact, that the laws of natural justice press upon us and demand such sharing of ourselves with our neighbors.

If this sounds too much like impractical preachment, then you probably are not the one who should seriously embark on the endeavors which serve this need. However, if your spine has been touched, to tingle just a little toward those people out there who need you, bless you for your kindness. They will bless you for any action you find it possible to take. Surely we cannot miss by even the ounce, the pound or the ton that which we are able and willing to share.

Let no one who feels unsuited or uninterested be the least bit self-conscious if this is not his cup of tea. Retirement is a very personal thing—a personal time.

It has been said that some people take no care of their money until they come to the end of it. Others do the same with their time, their talent, their energy and their expectations.

If it ever was important in your life, it is important now that you avoid withdrawing from circulation. That you fight to stay off the shelf. That you husband and harness all of your resources toward your own chosen goal of a healthy and happy retirement time of life.

Go back once more to your own personal resource inventory.

Make an inventory of yourself as a person. Set down pros and cons. List what you can do and what you can't do. Decide if you would like to, or are able to sell or not sell. To do or not do some particular other interesting thing. Check into old skills and new skills and don't dismiss them as old-fashioned. Do a hobby and job history on yourself. Smoke out what's saleable in you. This is a part of your own personal net worth—your own personal resource reservoir.

Stop selling yourself short at this time in your life. You can use all the positive personal power you can muster—to build up your own inventory of the personal assets which will help fulfill your own retirement expectations.

REHEARSE BEFORE YOU RETIRE 155

How well does your retirement inventory add up? Most of us will be amazed at all the human and material resources we possess.

ACTION IDEAS TO THINK ABOUT:

Let's count your money—your income to retire on. How much will you need? How much will you have?
AGE: *When you expect to retire* _____
TIME LEFT: *How many years to go/to earn?* _____
YEARS OF SERVICE: *Company pension years?* _____
What income will you expect to receive?

    Monthly? _____ $ _____
    Annually? _____ $ _____

  From which sources?
  Social Security? _____ $ _____
  Pension/retirement pay? _____ $ _____
  Retirement Trust? _____ $ _____
  Annuity? _____ $ _____
  Other insurance (not term)?
    Cash values you could acquire? _____ $ _____
  Interest/Dividends? _____ $ _____
  Rents/Royalties/Fees? _____ $ _____
  Other savings (beyond emergencies)? _____ $ _____
  Business income (earnings/buy and sell)? ___ $ _____
  Severance pay? _____ $ _____
  Inheritances expected? _____ $ _____
  Part-time work? _____

  WHAT DOES IT ALL ADD UP TO? _____ $ _____
    (*Move these figures*
    to top of page)

Now, what are you going to do about the Gap that remains between what you expect and what you need? What Gap-bridging is possible for you?

5

Set Your Own Retirement Timetable

MOST people actually have more of a choice about what happens in their lives than they believe they have. Most people are able, if they look and work ahead, to alter and accommodate to their own wishes and needs the time when they will retire.

Social Security and company retirement pension programs seem to have established age 65 as the cutoff point. Most people must retire, from most jobs and most companies, by that time. Recent changes in pension and social welfare programs acknowledge that some may wish to retire earlier. Age 62 has been set as another bench mark—with benefits diminished to some degree but not too punitively.

Some trends of the future indicate that age 60, or even less, may become—or may already be—the accepted retirement launching day. It really doesn't matter when they impose it on us if we insist that we remain in charge of that part of our lives.

When Will Retirement Happen to You?

Lucky you if you still have time to do more rehearsing; checking again things to try; places to sample; leftover steps to take; extra income you may still make. But—don't put it off forevermore. Be a bit itchy to get scratching.

These factors have a bearing on "when":

When your pension becomes sufficiently vested.	Year: ____
When Social Security is ready for you (62-65).	Year: ____
When your mortgage is close to being paid up.	Year: ____
When your kids are finishing their schooling.	Year: ____
When spouse is ready for Social Security.	Year: ____
When Annuities are paid-up or ready to pay out.	Year: ____
When your Wills, other legal matters are tidy.	When?____
When you know what else you want to do.	When?____
When you have settled on where you'll live.	When?____
When you've had it—or feel like "dropping-out"	When?____
When you've decided to start a new career.	When?____

There are lots of good reasons for quitting while you are ahead. For retiring early. Just to be retired, to do what you always wanted to do, to have a lot more time to do nothing—if that's what you have yearned for. To begin a new career or take partial employment. To travel, to visit around and to grow in new ways.

To jump into some new task or some new field in which you have always yearned to be. To begin to earn new money in a new way. To dedicate yourself to others—if that pathway is affordable and attractive to you.

Reasons for retiring early might include time to dream new dreams. To move out of the frantic pace, back into the human race, if that part of your life has been bugging you. To permit you to make new associations in new places, at a new pace, for better reasons than the habits which have become ingrown within us.

Actually you might want to begin earlier the task of readying yourself for a fuller retirement time of life by sharpening neglected skills, by harnessing hobbies and turning them into economic realities. Just to save the rest of your life for yourself.

After your family obligations have been taken care of—and after you have invested vigorously of yourself in your chosen work for 30 or 40 years—it does not seem a selfish determination to want to quit. To begin again at something new, or to

REHEARSE BEFORE YOU RETIRE

move over quietly into that promised land of having plenty of time—for a change.

You may often have wondered why you stayed on in such an unpredictable and unsatisfactory climate. Why you have remained among your own particular human parade—of friends, relatives and associates so long. Why not live somewhere new, in more relaxed circumstances, in a pleasanter climate, in a place which is geared to a slackening of all those energetic years.

I can promise you that nothing will happen to improve your retirement span of years or to increase their number and improve their quality more than taking some preparation steps now. If you sit around waiting for retirement to arrive, for it to happen to you, you will be less ready than you ought to be.

Reflect on the amount of planning thought and time you have often given to special vacation trips. Certainly this is true for any overseas trips which are taken. Consider how long you contemplated before you changed jobs, changed houses or moved from one part of your community to another. Most often it took years to set everything straight in advance.

We are approaching, here, the possibility that you are preparing to face another 10, 15 or 20 years—or as much as a quarter century—in that blessed time of life that comes after all of your work is done. Recent longevity records indicate that people may soon be living as long in retirement as they lived in their learning years or their working lifetime. It is also available to us to live healthier and happier lives in retirement. To go more places, to see and do more things. We appear, furthermore, to be able to afford more of these expectations and these realizations.

It will not do you any useful service to miss being ready—and on time.

Why not chart your own timetable? Put it on paper. Write down your age goal for retirement, and the year. This simple exercise tells you how many years you have left—for "rehearsing to retire."

You say the choice is not totally yours but depends as much on others.

Maybe you think your company's pension programs are not geared to those wayward souls among us who want to wander off before all the work is done. You may be afraid to face the entire uncertain business before it's absolutely necessary. Take heart, these preparation pressures are intended to be helps. Practical help for those who are too timid to tamper with life's timetables—to live and hesitate as if all were predestined for us.

We met a lady golfer at a "ladies day event" at one of those growing communities along Florida's gulf coast. We asked whether she and her husband had retired there, so that both of them could play more golf, on more days, in this more accommodating climate.

She said that they had come to live in Florida away from the cold and wintry days of the upper Midwest. They had not retired. She said they still had two children in school. The kids were picked up by bus near their home each day and taken to school. Her husband worked at a business related to his experience up North. They had simply come here, liked what they saw and decided to settle here.

Had they retired early? Not exactly. They had decided to come where they could enjoy themselves during more of the year. Doing more of the things they liked to do—boating, swimming and golfing. They decided that even if they earned less dollars here, and even if living costs were about the same as back home, they expected their lives to be inevitably lengthened. They claimed to be happier and felt that the added pressures and rewards back home would not guarantee them what they were already realizing from this new relaxed and rewarding experience.

Another family in another of these southern developments had come from Connecticut where the father had been both carpenter and builder. They had come south on one of those airborne scouting trips to examine this kind of corporate community living. They had found it so much to their liking that they stayed. He works as a carpenter and builder where they now live. Part of their housing costs are earned by showing other visitors through their own home. It's a demonstration sample. Their college-age son finished high school in their new land. He professes to miss little of his old life and their old home up north. He has found so much that is new and exciting in the south. None of them can any longer imagine why they should not have come or why they shouldn't have stayed.

Not every family is suited or ready for this much change. But more are ready than may realize it. They needn't go only to sunshine country. Many might prefer the Maine coast. Or the vast and glorious grandeur of the great Northwest with its mountains, forests and seacoast. Or the quiet of a rolling inland mountain meadow, the valley lands one finds in New Hampshire and Vermont. These would delight plenty of retiring families.

What's the matter with right where you are? You've always enjoyed living there. Contacts are all around. Friends and family are handy. You are relatively happy together. What about retiring right there? According to your own timetable and not according to timetables imposed on you by welfare agency decisions, by pension programs or by the pressure of relatives and friends. Your own timetable. According to your own attitudes.

To establish a sensible timetable one must take into consideration his own age and that of his wife. Other important factors include such things as your wife's and your own status with regard to Social Security, with regard to variations which may be possible in pension payments. Do you have any

REHEARSE BEFORE YOU RETIRE

school responsibilities left? Have these been anticipated or are they manageable wherever you may be, whenever you may retire? Finally, do the size of your dollars match your retirement ambitions—and your timetable?

Checker players do better if they plan those upcoming moves which are still five jumps ahead just as one would successfully ford a shallow stream by anticipating which rock to jump to next—which after that—in advance as much as possible.

Timetables can be anticipated too. We know a sales supervisor of a large national company who travels over most of a midwestern state in his work. He is representative of many other businessmen we've learned of in recent times. He and his wife vacation at a place they like, which is located on a lake. They are slowly acquiring property there and making the payments out of present income. Not only are they acquiring a place for themselves to live when his retirement time arrives—but they are also adding guest cabins for use now by friends and family, and for later rental income from other summer "visitors."

Our young friends plan to have eight of these units. If it turns out instead to be only five or six it won't matter as long as they find satisfaction and security in having things to do, with income to live on and with an operation that promises to meet their retirement expectations.

There are many ways to set up your own

timetable for retirement. Ted, the head of an accounting firm in our town, arranged his timetable in typical mathematical fashion. I have always envied his method and delight in sharing how he did it. This astute accountant set up the sale and transfer of his business to his employees and this put "his boys" into what had been his business.

They formed a corporation and bought him out at the rate of 10 per cent per year over a period of 10 years. They chose a leader from among their number and kept right on running the same accounting establishment under the same name. The former head man also began immediately the process of phasing himself out of his company at the rate of 10 per cent per year. In 10 years he was completely retired without having upset the company's clients and without having been an undue psychological or fiscal burden for too long. Their increasing interest in the company increased their need for added returns and this great plan made it all painlessly possible.

I am convinced that creative types may not have that kind of sensible logic. They may be more likely to miss this delightful way to dispose of a business and to phase out of a life's working schedule—into a gradual retirement on such a planned basis. In any event, Ted did it. Ted made it work and he has lived some 10 or 15 years past his carefully charted retirement date. Not a bad way to work it all out. To enable yourself to dispose of a costly business. To help your associates acquire it. To give you income, on a lessened scale to match your lessening contribution. And to take your sales price out as capital gains income—as you need it.

That's setting your own retirement timetable. It's about the best plan I've seen.

There are other ways. A dentist we've heard about moved his practice from a semi-metropolitan center to the banks of a trout stream upstate in one of the watered Midwestern states. It's inaccurate to say that he moved his practice. But he took his equipment and established his relocated practice in the office attached to his new shoreland home. He began the process of seeking out those dental cases which appealed to him especially and which challenged his particular skills. We understand he's not too busy with dentistry to let it interfere with his fishing. We also understand that he doesn't spend all of his time fishing though he can wet a line any time he chooses. Meanwhile he and his wife have a lovely life with a lovely view, with new neighbors, and with a lessened pace. Doc Yank didn't do this exactly as a part of retirement. His plan included a special dental extraction service, providing privacy along with excellent clinical service. Patients live anonymously—in a cabin on the stream—fish for trout while their mouths heal and while they are being fitted for new dentures. Doc took this relaxed route, midterm in his professional life. He probably added both a pleasanter life and longer time to really live besides.

Timetables won't wait for retirees who face their deadlines without being sure whether they have enough money or not. It's an old and normal concern to wonder if one will have enough security. It might be well to check this out with those who have gone into retirement before you, to find out in impersonal ways, how much it takes to live—per month and per year of your remaining retirement years. Match this to your net worth chart. Add your pension and welfare resources and see how the figures match up. Perhaps you're better off than you had expected. Many are.

Do you think you're too young to quit? That you need not concern yourself with timetables at this time? It may be true for you. Our question is not who quits. Rather it concerns those who count up their choices and decide accordingly. Timetables help us build better plans.

Your friends, family and associates—should you be foolish enough to ask for their opinion—will have lots of advice. You're too young to quit. Where did this kind of foolish notion come from? These are the same people who will stand sadly at your bier, remembering how hard you worked and for how long. How you should have taken it easier sooner. Listen to your own drummer and march off at the head of your own parade—in anticipation of a great new life.

So you're afraid to be thought old—and fin-

REHEARSE BEFORE YOU RETIRE

ished? Better to be old than finished off. Better to work it all out in advance according to a well-planned schedule than to come up against the day and deed—in a panic. You may not want to retire any sooner than necessary because you are afraid of boredom. If that's how you respond, it's probably the way you should plan.

So many people we've known have taken their retirement by taking a step at a time. I know several who have turned their professional skills into teaching careers. One runs the business school division of one of his former university's state-wide centers. Another, a former sales manager, teaches distributive education to vocational and technical school students. They bring actual examples and case method demonstrations of the experience it would take years to acquire from text book teachers.

These "new career people" make a real contribution and the pay they collect has improved meanwhile to make it even more worthwhile. They may have sacrificed immediate big league income but I doubt that it cost them too much in income sacrifice. Each of these testimonials reports that the wives have also responded to the new challenges and they have enjoyed a new prestige. The new creativity they are associated with stirs in them the right kind of healthy thankfulness for their good fortune.

Timetables can be hurried—or held back. We know of two or three successful business executives who quit their jobs and took their families along—to study theology in the training schools of their church denomination in order to prepare for congregational teaching and preaching. One of these went to Nigeria to do missionary work. All report a fulfillment beyond their hopes. They show a kind of assured satisfaction that makes you pleased they took this difficult step. The real heroes in such new careers are probably the wives and the families who go along. In the end, however, they all benefit from their sacrifice. The time comes in this timetable dialogue to take another test. It's a simple one question test but the answer is important to you.

"HOW READY ARE YOU TO RETIRE?"

If your unfinished work-a-day tasks, your incomplete economic circumstances and your unready psychological platform are still out of step with this consideration of timetables, don't be alarmed. Better to face these facts now, to give you added time to catch up with unsolved shortcomings.

For example, you might wish to get a part-time job, even before you retire, in order to learn a skill. To gain confidence, to pick up a few dollars and to make connections. To prove to your wife that you know how to solve such future problems. She may wish to find her own answer to her own concerns about boredom or lessened income by taking a part-time job herself—as a receptionist or a check-out attendant in a supermarket. Or in a choice from

REHEARSE BEFORE YOU RETIRE

among dozens of other ways in which she can earn an added dollar or two to fill the days and to prove that there are many ways to keep busy. To keep earning, to enrich one's life and to meet new people. To assure each other that wherever we may go we will have the means to do with and the challenge with which to fill our days.

Many, many of the families who approach retirement—whether they are ready or not—must also face the fact that they will have less income. Fortunately, they will probably also have lessened appetites and lessened needs. We might as well face those facts in advance so that changes can be made. Changes in cost of living to match earnings and savings.

It's tough to advise others which of these steps come first because they all come so close together. One problem leads to the need for still another answer. Another answer points up another problem. Today most of us can get some kind of part-time employment. We can prove it to ourselves by spending vacations where we think we might wish to live. Try lining up jobs in a variety of the branch situations which today's distribution and service industries provide.

We have previously considered using vacations for rehearsing for retirement. One of the best ways to make the most of such vacation time is to use those days to plan for first-hand experience in "walking through" your own retirement timetable.

With a week of your vacation, take just such step-by-step, day-by-day dry runs. It's good practice and it's refreshing to find so many things you can do for different kinds of companies who need your special kind of help. The more you make sure you are retiring *to* something, the more you have an inventory of all of your personal resources—personal, material and psychological—the more you will be setting up a sound timetable. A variety of very good things will surely result and you will acquire the added comfort of the confidence you gain this way.

Not only will you be getting ready for the time which will surely come. Many will discover—in spirit and in fact—that they are already at that point in life, and in their circumstances, which will permit them to take steps to move into partial retirement any time they please.

It's a sensible step toward practical independence. To know exactly where the next rock is—ready for our next jump. To know what choices of moves exist on our life's checkerboard. Look back into the experience of some of the other folks we have visited in these reports. Remember Harry and his doctor's prescription to find a brand new city along his daily pathway? How he found a new life up there? New opportunities and new job offers which helped him retire earlier than he had dared to hope.

Remember Sam, the piano-tuning man. He set his own timetable. He equipped himself to meet it. To save his threatened health and to please both

REHEARSE BEFORE YOU RETIRE

his wife and himself. He became useful in the piano-tuning business and was able to relocate just where he pleased—doing as much as he wished of what he liked best to do.

There were the mushroom people who collected, catalogued and photographed them and who wrote of the lore of their mushroom finds. Now they find themselves in the business of lecturing, showing their slides to audiences throughout the country. They became authorities and gained their independence. They made their timetable out of small circumstances. They ended up in charge of their problem. The doctor who was the camera buff and a student of photography stepped from one career to a slower-paced one to keep him busy and happy. Selling, teaching and demonstrating how to take better pictures. He provides a real service and is enjoying a real satisfaction. Other friends and acquaintances are building their own island in the sun. They go there on vacation and add a board or two—or a room or two—establishing their own vacation paradise where they wish it to be.

We've examined so many ways in which so many wonderful people have helped themselves over their hump of uncertainty with regard to that nagging nuisance many consider the problems of retirement.

There is another delightful tale which involves both husband and wife. These good people earned their progress in their company. Then they were transferred for the last three working years of his career to his company's home office in New York City. This enabled them to partake in abundance of the museums, the art centers, the plays and concerts they had always yearned to haunt. They reveled in their new opportunity. Even this was not enough. The wife was interested in handwriting analysis. She took a course in graphology. She became quite expert on the subject and being a verbal person, was quickly able to blend her substantial new found skill and knowledge with her ability to write and tell of it in an interesting way. Now she gives selected lectures, demonstrations and meeting programs on the subject to the growing number who have taken an interest in this scientific study. She has also been called in as expert by the courts and other legal agencies to give her professional opinion on handwriting considerations.

Meanwhile, he is retired. Occasionally he accepted an advisory job or two—a consulting assignment now and again—a creative task which pleases him. He keeps busy and keeps his talent challenged. He keeps tuned in with his colleagues in the business. Between both their fascinations they perhaps add a dollar or two to their psychic pile—whether this has any importance or not. The very fact of being able to pick up some extra income probably does more to bolster people's halting egos at such times than all of the fine words friends might lavish on them.

REHEARSE BEFORE YOU RETIRE 173

It can really be important at retirement time to know that you are doing well whatever it is you are doing. To have someone pay you even a pittance proves that you can still do something useful and important.

A special point should probably be made about timing—in the light of setting timetables for retirement. Many men work hard at getting ahead but not all of them arrive at their peak at the same time in life. Some get there earlier and some never reach the heights. Each touches his own zenith in his own time and in his own way. Some men give up trying because they feel the deck is stacked against them. They are sure they've gone as far as they can. Office politics. The boss's son. New people brough in through mergers. All kinds of reasons.

It's sad to see men who have made it well enough begin the process of going downhill—hanging on to their old job for another year, for another piece of pension pie—to try to add another gold brick to their unfinished retirement pile.

Lots of other people feel it's important to phase out or quit when they are at or near their peak—or have begun to pass it. There is something sensible to be said for hanging on to your working lifetime reputation and your own self-respect by quitting a little early. To try something new, something you will probably do better because it's fresh and fits your special personal skills, something that can't be measured against your past record because you haven't been there before.

It is pathetic for the families involved and for friends and associates to witness the has-been who stayed too long, where time had passed him by. The guy who once had it made but who goes sour may either blame himself self-pityingly or he may try to hang the blame for his luckless lot on others.

How are your nerves? How's your psyche? These are important manly and human factors which have a strong influence on your retirement timetable. Is your nerve faltering—is your psyche sagging? It's well to know yourself and for your wife to know her mate—for both to know each other's limits.

If you happen to be part of a company where you are building an increasing equity, have you made arrangements for cashing in such equity on some kind of income-spreading plan? On a tax-saving basis? To set up assured and secured income so that your widow doesn't end up being your partner's unwelcome new partner thereby risking the loss of much of what you have worked for?

Perhaps you own real estate which is increasing in value or land or forest property where growth has occurred. Why hang on to these too long if their values are needed to provide the means for you to step into freedom? Become your own man and adjust your retirement timetable if that is your inclination.

Perhaps you can sell your equity on a phas-

REHEARSE BEFORE YOU RETIRE

ing-out basis, on a schedule fitted to your needs and to your company's circumstances. Perhaps you would like to leave a little in as seed money for future growth. It's time to consider the pleasant problem of enjoying some of the fruits of what you've worked for and accumulated before you lose the ability to spend saved money. Or to lose the ability to enjoy the spending of it.

For some men it may be best to run when they have it nearly made—especially if they have some fierce and burning spirit—some place to go, something else to do, to set some brand new worlds on fire. Go before you lose that spark. Before your head of steam blows away.

Once again, as in the matter of the inventory of your personal resources, you may need encouragement that you can indeed make it out there without steady drudgery, without a regular paycheck. A few more suggestions:

Check in with Manpower, or with one of the other extra and part-time help agencies. You may be surprised at the wide variety of services Manpower provides and needs. Somebody like you brings each of these skills and know-how to these firms. Why not let it be you—why not become part of their service inventory. Then you can work as much as you like, when you want to. If you want to. Some folks like the idea of moving to new places. Traveling overseas. Perhaps even living there.

There are jobs for specialists, especially retired specialists, in "temporary career" situations abroad. Many can be arranged for right here at home through the State Department. Or through the United Nations or various church and welfare agencies. The information services of these agencies can be found by checking with the reference department of your public library.

A word about libraries. Much of the general public has too limited an idea of how extensive are their services and how helpful public libraries can be. Libraries have books to expand knowledge, to entertain and fill leisure hours. Beyond this, libraries have reference data for any field you can imagine. There are other strange and interesting helps as well. Most libraries maintain sections on investing, special collections on real estate laws and regulations. Estate planning, trusts and so on.

Libraries also have current telephone books of most major cities whose yellow pages are filled with facts to stir your dreams. They list embassies, consulates, agencies and associations. There are also volumes listing foundations and the associations for these might show you the way to go, to settle down in some new place overseas—or in our southern hemisphere where the living is cheaper, the pace slower, where your dollars go further and the need is greater for your interest and contribution.

Anyone who has a normal amount of human relationship talent can do some kind of selling. This goes for him—or for her. Part-time sales help is

REHEARSE BEFORE YOU RETIRE 177

needed in shoe stores, camera and record departments, clothing stores, food stores and gift shops. You would be surprised how many places of business need desperately better help than that which comes up to wait on you now. Tell them why and how you are better. Offer to be Friday or Saturday relief help to show them how good you are. Work your way into a bigger part-time job if that is your aim.

Perhaps you are a modest tycoon with a string of houses or flats to rent—or with cottages at a lake. If you are a reasonable handy man, and if you have just enough of a hardened heart to ignore many of the murmurs about falling plaster and temperamental plumbing you can probably turn part of your spare time into extra income dollars. You can provide part of that extra income which makes it possible for you to quit while you are still ahead—or to get even further ahead.

It's true that planning, arranging, scheduling and developing timetables should have been begun last year or the year before that. It gets no better if you won't begin now.

Bear in mind that you will have less need for income *for one big reason*. When you don't work, and don't earn, you don't pay income tax. That's an item of 10 to 50 per cent depending upon your income level. It comes right off the top. While there are also other lessened needs for normal income, it still takes dollars to keep retirement times spinning pleasantly.

Most major cities list job-finding and skill-placing agencies. Most private or industrial organizations provide this service for company people. The thing to do is to write for data and to write right away.

We have just come back from visiting a string of gift shops in another lake resort area. It's amazing what these shops sell. What is even more interesting is where they get the merchandise. Not all of it is ground out in factories in Chicago or in Japan. Much is artsy-craftsy and is the result of a winter's work by otherwise not-regularly-employed persons.

People who are on vacation have set aside an attitude which is apparently loaded with dollars which burn holes in their take-home pockets. They have gifts to buy for Aunt Nellie and for all the cousins, neighbors and friends who need to be remembered. They indulge themselves and their children and look for new ideas. They seem to go right on buying a lot of stuff that is pretty junky and not inexpensive.

What can you make better than what you see offered? What can you create or produce which you have never seen for sale? Gift ideas which an increasing number of visitors anywhere would respond to with money and enthusiasm.

FINALLY, timetables like resource lists, are personal matters. No one can tell you what your circumstance is or which family factors may alter your dreamiest dreams. Some of us may need to hang in there longer because it's easier and less unpleasant to do this daily slugging in the plant or in the office than to save too much of it as take-home argument and warfare.

If the wife isn't ready and can't get ready for retirement her husband has some facts to face about these foolish notions he may have about checking out a little sooner. But nothing can obscure the fact that most of us are going to be cashiered out at age 60 or 62, or by 65 anyway. When that happens it doesn't matter too much to the world whether wifey dear is ready. It only matters to his and her world. If you are still some kind of man in your own house, *get her ready!* You've worked hard and provided well. She's done her share and you both deserve a chance to quit, without quibbling, if that is your mutual pleasure. So—sell her!

Finally, health and wealth are weighted factors on any scale that measures a man's working lifetime. We have whatever health we have. We possess whatever possessions we haven't frittered away. Add these to your social welfare status which you have been earning toward. Settle for that if that's the best you will be able to do.

And promise yourselves one more small favor! Promise you will have the personal self-kindness and self-assurance to enjoy that which has fallen to your lot. Chances are it will be about as much as you have been led to expect anyway. Whoever said there would be a golden fleece hanging as the watch fob on your golden retirement timepiece?

Timetables are no good at all except to indicate starting times, destinations and arrivals. Timetables are guides. They tell you *when to go.*

So go, good friend. Or stay if you must. But if you can go, go quietly and confidently. Accept your joyful pensioned retirement pastime as justice due.

You've earned it so plan to enjoy it!

ACTION IDEAS TO THINK ABOUT:

You are chairman of your own retirement clean-up committee. There's some simple but important housekeeping to do.

	Done	Still To Do
Like, getting family records straight	——	——
Getting group health coverage arranged for	——	——
Getting Social Security details lined up	——	——
Arranging company pension details	——	——
Making lists of family possessions	——	——
Updating an inventory of investments	——	——
Having wills brought up-to-date; for both	——	——

*Arranging for a family adviser on
fiscal matters* .... —— ——
*Checking out family health situation
with doctors.* .... —— ——
*Getting operations/treatments out of
the way* .... —— ——
*Getting as much "paid-up" as
possible—before.* .... —— ——
Having assets converted to income? .... —— ——
*Have you ever set down basic retirement
aims and ambitions you hope to realize?* . —— ——
*Do you know where you will begin
retirement?* .... —— ——

6

Expect To Enjoy Your Retirement

REMEMBER how it was when you were a child?

Each day was filled with joyful expectations. You awoke in the affirmative. You only expected to relish, to savor—to touch and be touched by each new experience. It may sound idyllic now but it was fun then. Life was full of high hopes. Promising of excitement. And you were filled with a vital vigor.

I dare say the first 15 or 20 years of your life had about the same fascination level as this. Later you probably became somewhat more realistic as the harder facts of life were imposed upon you. Life was still full of hope and ambition. Goals to reach and objectives to accomplish successfully.

Then along came those middle 30 to 40 years of our working and worrying life span. Each of us handled that period differently. We faced up to our responsibilities to love and provide for those we had accepted as our responsibility. Fortunately most of

REHEARSE BEFORE YOU RETIRE 183

Career Women—and Singles

Retirement rewards are available to all. And so are its uncertainties and disappointments. Much that has been suggested in these pages applies equally to men and women; either as couples or as singles. Each has the total task—and some have special problems.

Career women usually have greater flexibility but they may also feel locked-in by double-standard limitations.

Examining a few of these questions may help:

	Yes	No
Are you free to go—and live—anywhere?		
Can your retirement begin earlier?		
Do you have compelling reasons to stay on?		
Do others depend on your staying?		
Can you accept these "responsibilities"?		
Where would you rather be? Is there a dream?		
Why can't you just take off?		
Are you concerned about being alone too much?		
Do you easily make new friends? Will you try?		
Are you an adventurous person, ready to go?		
Do familiar old friends and family roots hold you—and is it really your preference to remain where you have these comforting anchors?		

us didn't quibble about the price. We just kept on going, doing and accomplishing as much as our abilities, our energies and our application merited. We arrived where we were going with as much "success" as we were willing and able—or fortunate enough—to bring along with us.

Now we are looking ahead to the final 15 to 25 years of our lives. Once more we should be blending in that wonderful ingredient of joyful expectation to the years that lie ahead. We have worked hard and fussed a great deal. We are what we are and there is not too much of great consequence that we can do to change it now. There is always room for some improvement and for a better adaptation to one's circumstance. The fact is, however, that we are facing toward the finishing goal line. Let's promise ourselves to face it in a friendly, cheerful and highly expectant frame of mind.

Whether you have earned it all or not—or whether you have made all the progress you hoped for—you will surely come to your retirement and it will be singularly yours. You can decide to be disappointed with it. Or, you can promise yourself, and more importantly, promise your spouse, that you are going to enjoy every wonderful minute of it. It has been said that life's last great gift to most of us is the freedom to live anew that releasing reward which comes with our pension and our escape from regular responsibility.

But you aren't quite finished yet! Regardless

REHEARSE BEFORE YOU RETIRE

of all you may have planned and all your good intentions, you still can mess up your retirement. We are assuming that you are still looking ahead to it and that you are still gainfully employed. Still meeting some kind of a work-a-day timetable of obligations. Here's how you can still louse it up.

One of the best ways to assure your failure is never to think about retirement—never to think ahead—as if that time will never come. Or, that you will not be able to bear it when it does come. If you remain troubled about that time of life, you are playing ostrich and will have deserved what ostriches must inevitably get. An eyeful of sand. If you suffer from the silly delusion that it's nobler to die with your boots on, you are not facing today's facts of American social welfare life.

Think about retirement joyfully as if you had a right to expect to enjoy it. You will then have a better chance that you will.

Another important way to insure catastrophe in retirement is to make no plans for it. Don't set any savings aside. Don't think about what you might want to retire *to*. Don't bother to inventory your resources and assets. Don't do any of those childish rehearsal routines which are being suggested. Who can live in the future when so much work still remains in the present? Relax. There will always be sufficient work.

Most of those who had made some plans for their retirement tell us that they had so much more to look forward to. So much more to accomplish and enjoy. They ended up with less than enough time to get the job all done.

Most suggest that we keep stressing that if they had known how wonderful it could be to be ready, and to retire, they would have done it earlier. They would have saved a little more of themselves and a lot more of life for fuller enjoyment. We do not necessarily believe that this is the only way everybody should do it. Some are not psychologically suited. Their choice must be on their very own. Planning just makes it go better.

Obviously, the facts of life in retirement are customarily built around less income. Most admit, however, that there is also a somewhat lessened need for spending money. This is not to say that inflation and the size of our poke will keep us as cozy as we have always been—a little short of all we'd like in resources—a little less than enough to enjoy everything to the full.

And yet, most retired people bequeath and deliver estate remainders which they were not able to live-up all by themselves. Estates that end up in state and federal tax coffers, and in the hands of attorneys, accountants and other capable and necessary administrators. Often it is passed on to ungrateful, quarreling relatives and even to fussing children. If folks could see some of the problems their unspent dollars leave behind they wouldn't worry so hard about having so much of it left over.

REHEARSE BEFORE YOU RETIRE

We do need to be prudent about sickness and family dependency in our later years. Circumstances which might make us a burden either to the state or to our children. People don't relish that idea. But today's welfare programs are fashioned to take care of more and more health and welfare needs in increasing ways. Some of us will not be "fat with fortune" in retirement, but most of us will live well enough—according to our normally accustomed circumstances.

If you insist on getting ready to mess up your own retirement, don't forget to keep your wife ignorant of your hopes, ambitions and intentions. You wouldn't want to stir her up unnecessarily, would you? Cunning of you to be "so thoughtful" of her by not including her in your plans. Actually, it's thoughtless and treacherous for you to avoid facing with your spouse the facts about retirement because, whether you face it or not, these facts are going to be facing both of you sooner than you wish or expect.

Even otherwise sensible women will admit that they duck facing unpleasant concerns like retirement by avoiding the realities which bring them into focus.

Most wives don't retire. They have just about everything left over when you retire that they ever had before. Except about ten times more of you and often less than half of the coin it takes to keep bodies and souls together.

Women worry that retirement may not be

any bed of roses unless they get a job. What if they become widowed? That doesn't leave them much of a choice. So the idea bothers them. It won't help any to put off all consideration until your retirement surprises you. Look at it together now. Have your first arguments now while you both have the good sense, the good humor and the good health to get past those first few tears.

Finally, you can practically guarantee that retirement will be a messed-up time of life if you approach it and go into it expecting to not enjoy it.

Man may have been made for work—to work until someone else pulls the plug. Sure—there's so much left to do. So much the world needs that you can still do. But isn't it a monumental arrogance to assume that you're the last guy responsible to help get it all done?

There's a touch of puritanism in us all which makes it seem sinful to think of goofing off. Irresponsible, improvident and unfair to those who rely on us for support and sustenance. Employers establish welfare programs and pension plans for their people and yet these very systems keep whipping wayward dreamers into line.

Some sociologists believe that it's highly creative for those who are suited to it—for those who feel they would like to take a new look at problems which are new to them, and to which they can apply old and familiar skills—to quit early. To create new

REHEARSE BEFORE YOU RETIRE 189

careers, to gain new rewards and earn new money. To realize a lot of new satisfactions.

I don't remember that there was anything in the Ten Commandments, or in the marriage contract either, that stipulated how long you had to keep your nose to that grindstone. How long you have to keep those heavy boots on. To demonstrate all that dreary and endless responsibility.

If you won't plan and if you won't talk about it; if you can't save for retirement and if you don't expect to enjoy it, excuse this intrusion, this distraction. If you are satisfied to let your spirit be sapped away by a few more fast trips around the track, promise to look the other way while some among us sneak off a little early, a touch furtively perhaps, to peer into retirement's promised land. Over the fence figuratively and literally.

No one will thank you if you mess up the retirement time of your life. If you aren't going to earn any credit for lousing it up, you'd better avoid the certain blame—by doing something about it now.

It seems simpler when examining abstract propositions to take a step by step approach, to reason it out logically. That's what we have been doing here, examining six simple factors which will help you to retire more successfully.

It doesn't take much judgment to evaluate the difference between arriving at the time when you will be out of work—or, to begin instead a pleasant and practical program of retiring *to* something.

Perhaps there's a new career for you. To try new skills, earn new money, to accomplish new things and to help new people in new ways. Perhaps it's just a partial career to fill our lives with some involvement, some earnings to help extend our savings. Perhaps it's wishing to try again in a new way to add to life in a new environment.

There's promise in meeting new people and seeing new places. But it remains only a promise for some. Others may wish to linger among familiar friends and circumstances. Each must do it his own way. Each may also do some experimenting among some of the other ways, to make certain that we are choosing the best possible pathway for ourselves.

For some, retirement is intended to be, and probably should be, a totally relaxing regimen of not too much to do besides loafing. Letting the rest of the world go by. Who can say that's wrong? It's a reward, isn't it?

Wasn't the time for life's accomplishments back there in the past somewhere? Whether we made it or not matters little now.

Doubtless, many can find, and should seek, opportunities to share themselves with those who need them. There's so much that needs doing, so many who need us just as we are. We may not know them now and they may not know us. But the twain

REHEARSE BEFORE YOU RETIRE

can indeed still meet and each should gain from the encounter.

We've said it often before. It isn't a question of whether to retire so much as it is a question of when. Add quickly the where and the how. That's what this examination is all about.

Examining how to retire brings with it a word of warning. We are reminded of going-away parties which celebrated and honored young men leaving to serve their country. With gifts and plaudits lavished in loving ways upon them. Only to find in embarrassment later that the decision of the military may have rejected the state of their health. It always felt touchingly sad to see them come back with their expected military mission unaccomplished.

We make the same point about men marching off into retirement. That's why we take a rather dim view of glorified gold-watch retirement parties which send men off with ceremony, with some real and many crocodile tears, into the confused arms of concerned wives—unprepared, unrealistically and unsatisfactorily retired.

A PARTNER in an eastern service organization told his people he was going off on a long vacation. He then went into his retirement with only his very top boss knowing that he was taking his final leave. We know a dentist who fiddled around with the idea of retiring for a year or two before making the final break. When he did quit, he did exactly that. He simply didn't go back to the office any more and advised his patients to seek other services. The abruptness may have puzzled some of those concerned, but it kept the entire subject from being talked to death. From being killed with high promises and poor delivery.

Those who have wandered off most quietly into deserved pastures seem to have found them greener than some others we've known who celebrated too much their "second coming."

Let's dream a little about what you might do in the early part of your retirement—while you are in the process of establishing a new set of routines which you and your wife can live with. Do you have extensive family connections scattered around the country? Aunts, uncles and cousins you have seldom, if ever seen? It's silly to wait until they gather at your bier—or expect you at theirs.

Families, after all, are still an important part of the fabric of social life in our society. Today they are often scattered and out of touch with each other. They come together at weddings or funerals and belatedly admit to the need they feel for keeping alive this bridge to past heritages.

Some who are approaching retirement may have branches of their family in foreign lands. What better way to learn of these customs and cultures— or to share something of ours with them? To go for what may turn out to be the first of several visits with them. We say several because once this travel

REHEARSE BEFORE YOU RETIRE 193

bridge is crossed and the contact has begun, you'll find them wanting to visit you in return. To have their children visit you in search of a greater understanding between our lands—all woven together through the solid fabric of family trust.

There are many other reasons why you might wish to travel to faraway places. Perhaps as a younger person you dreamed of what life would be like in the South Pacific, in Australia or in Scandinavian or Arctic countries where the sun seldom sets or seldom rises.

To tread with trepidation in troubled historic harbor cities where civilization had its beginning and where it seems again to be troubling about tomorrow.

Travel for most who try it opens so many new horizons and shows so many new ways to relate to new people that it simply can't be over-emphasized for most of you. They do things differently in different lands. Not necessarily less well or better. Just differently!

Seeing helps one's understanding and it extends knowledge elaborately. You'll find that people everywhere have similar fears, dreams and hopes. They raise families and face the future—even a future with their own kind of retirement—with about the same degrees of confusion, uncertainty or hope which we bring to our own. If you plan to go abroad anywhere, learn just a few words of the language of the people you will visit. You will feel such a great satisfaction that you will probably find it difficult to move on to all of the other places where your remaining resources should take you.

Do not be surprised if after a first visit you should wish to settle in Mexico, in Greece, in Ireland or in any of such similarly fascinating places. This is not to say that all of you would prefer living there to where you had always been. It's just that it's so different, so fascinating and usually inexpensive. One finds that dollars stretch further in many of these places if one is willing to live in circumstances similar to those which were probably not normal back home. Circumstances which are, however, appropriate to this time and circumstance of life.

Be prepared for differences and welcome them if you go. There is a growing community of retired Americans living in various friendly communities in Mexico and other central American countries. This is also true of many of the European countries and particularly in a lot of the Caribbean Islands.

But not all of us want to live so far away. Some won't even go there to have a look. Others are satisfied to stay closer to the familiar, to avoid getting overtired, to skip the surprised tummy syndrome that sometimes comes with unfamiliar places, with eating new foods and experimenting with new fancies.

Some should stay home. This is not to say they are more right or wrong. The point here is only

REHEARSE BEFORE YOU RETIRE

that the possibility be considered by each family. Whether one is rich or poor doesn't matter so much. Usually we are relatively accustomed to our lot in life. That may be mostly good. To accept what we have, that which we cannot change. This is wisdom—an essential for happiness.

It might be well to go back—to re-examine the guarantee we promised earlier as you began planning for successful retirement. This is the guarantee that relates to rehearsing before you retire. Too much fuss can't be made of this simple, sensible fact. It gives you the how-to and the how-not-to answers. It helps you shape up your list of do's and don'ts, to help assure maximum success when you take on retirement full time.

Rehearsing tells you from experience where in the world you should set up your rocking chair. It tells something about the speed at which you would like to rock and which direction you would like to have your rocker pointed. Perhaps yours shouldn't be a stationary platform. Why not have it mounted on a drifting raft that takes off some Tuesday for a many-thousand mile tour of the unfamiliar and uncharted byways in your future. Put it on skiis or on a surfboard and point it anywhere fascinating.

It's well to face realities on matters as personal and potentially problematic as one's retirement. We've seen people sitting on sunbathed benches along the entire gulf coastline from New Orleans to the top of Florida. Some do it positively, constructively, happily. Others sit around disconsolately, putting in their time. We've seen them stare equally vacantly at arriving airplanes, at lovely palm-lined verandas and at sunny shopping plazas.

Roam on down to the courthouse in any city in any part of the country and you'll see more of the same. Some people have limited personal resources. That's the way they are and for them that is probably enough. Others bring along too few things to care strongly about. Things of interest to fill their days with fascination.

If there is one common denominator that seems to shine in those who are most pleasantly busy it is the joyful going from one task to another, from one activity and one place to another—all an evolutionary part of what doesn't even seem like retirement. Perhaps these people had similar resource strength in their busy and productive working lifetimes.

We think of one grand and lovely lady who formerly operated a Midwestern retail business. She now lives and works part-time at a plush Western inn. It is difficult to keep track of where she's at during her time off—in sunny California. Where she is anywhere in the entire country—as she moves around here and there to visit friends, to be with her children when they need her or just in enjoying their lives with them. She works a little and makes still more new friends. She earns a little money and pays her own way. She brought along most of her own

REHEARSE BEFORE YOU RETIRE

resources but we note that she keeps replenishing these—both her financial and her psychological resources.

We know another—an early retiree—a vigorous and successful advertising professional who ran his own company in Latin America and in the islands. Upon the sale of these establishments to a large metropolitan agency, he moved himself and his family back to his wife's home town. Here he plays golf and participates in much that concerns his new community.

They say he runs the country club. I'm satisfied he doesn't run it for any personal gain or out of any boredom either. He's involved and enjoys this change in his life. I am only aware of one occasion when he seriously considered taking on renewed promotional assignments. I know nothing of his resources except those which I can observe. I think he was 52 when he began the process of living a new life in a new way in this new place. His friends tell me he's wearing it all extremely well and happily. That he's a great asset to his community.

Remember to be sensible about the degree to which you are willing to commit yourself to new activities in retirement. Some programs are too vigorous and too costly in energy for your reduced reserves, your available time. For the reduced income one finds in retirement jobs. Your future usefulness and the pleasures for which you will now have more time carry a price. Each of us must make sure that he can afford to pay that price.

We're told that one way to help assure the success of the husband-wife retirement syndrome is for the couple to establish he and she hobbies. Things they can do together. We know of several who have become expert in hand-gun marksmanship, who traveled and completed in nearby states. Skills like these hold high interest for some. Collectors of coins and stamps seem endlessly to be visiting among each other—talking and collecting. Shells are a great fascination for many who sit and contemplate—or who stir about faraway beaches to bring back fascinating sea-going specimens. Some become rock collectors who may later turn into gem cutters.

One of the nicest stories about the heaven which retirement can be, has to do with a dear old friend who is really not so old. This man has written plays. He plays and enjoys music of all kinds. He had worked in personnel and industrial relations for a large company and retired at an age that seemed appropriate. I do not know at what exact age he quit working.

He and his wife left children behind. They visit them about once a year. I have noticed that their grandchildren sometimes also go back and forth. What have these resourceful people done with all their new-found time, about all of their intense involvement in life?

Kenneth began learning to play the cello

REHEARSE BEFORE YOU RETIRE

since he retired. He became skilled enough to play in his area's symphony. It sounds phenomenal but it points the way for what one can do. He also reads and writes. Together, they find just about everything interesting. It must have taken Kenneth an abnormal quota of determined energy to become sufficiently competent on the cello to fit into his orchestrated regimen. All of this he learned while he was well into his 60's.

What is even more wonderful is how fondly he writes about their life in retirement. A most beloved time to them because they can do exactly as they please. To do as much as they can manage to squeeze into their days—and out of their energy. Kenneth can't sell the blessings of purposeful retirement highly enough. We find this to be the not uncommon and most wonderful bonanza of what could surely become an empty period at the lagging end of life for those who neglect to plan for it.

Regardless of your age or your attitude toward planning for retirement, do some specific things to help you decide what you might really like to do. What needs doing? Go to visit senior citizen centers. Sit and chat with the men and women who participate there. Ask about their lives. Where had they lived? What had they done for a living? Learn about their hobbies or lack of them.

Ask impersonal questions about how much money it takes to fulfill the needs and wants of a normal retirement span. Offer to take those less privileged where they wish to go. To visit an arboretum. A flower show, an art show or a concert. To hear visiting scholars at area colleges or universities. Relate in some personal way to a few of these people over a period of time. Offer your help to the director of the center—to take someone home with you for a meal or an occasional visit. Pick one or two of the less favored and bring a little joyful caring to a few of the less prepared of the center's habitues.

Get close to some of these people. Regardless of your age or that they may be seventy or eighty, pick out the more interesting from among them and set your own dialogue. Find out what you need to know to help with what they may want to know. Seek answers that concern and trouble you.

Benefits will flow both ways. They will be pleased to have their days and hours filled with human kindness—they will appreciate your concern. You will learn to observe and will come to understand what your own future might be like not too many years hence. From their experiences and from their observations, you can learn to look ahead better, to plan more resourcefully. To rehearse better, to really retire *to* something. It's an act of kindness that pays both ways. One assumes that such visits would not be only self-seeking. That could be a kind of unkindness.

We know this sincere learning and rehearsing approach works. We have done it, visiting with the regulars who come to these senior citizen centers and

REHEARSE BEFORE YOU RETIRE 201

with the volunteers who provide the activities to fill idle hours. The nice thing about senior citizen centers is that they are getting established most everywhere—wherever people are. They may not exist in very small communities but they are increasing in number according to need and population concentrations.

When you have sufficiently embarked upon definite hobbies or avocational preoccupations, it might be well to set up certain target projects to accomplish. Goals for you to shoot at now—while you have the choice to make changes should one activity pale and another please you more.

Why not pick from three to five tough assignments? Structure how you expect to come to grips with these several ambitions, interests, activities or projects.

If you're troubled about what such a list should include, and if you are not sure just what these interests might involve, go to the reference people in your local public library. Delve into their resources. Tell them as candidly as you care to what your purpose and plan is. If you don't want to do this in your local community, go to the library at a local college or university if these are available to you. Or go to libraries in neighboring cities.

Still another fascinating route is open to you if you get in touch with local employment advisory services, with psychological testing facilities which might exist in your area.

Be careful not to approach ideas like these with grimness. Bring with you instead the lighthearted indifference that is reminiscent of your youth. Put together from your inventory of resources some goals which relate your know-how to the need which others have for your company or for some small loving comfort. For little touches of a happier, more human involvement with people.

Find out how you can bring some real hope to those who live hopeless lives. Set forth on a program of learning how to love the unloved and the unlovable. Your abundance of aptitude and experience can be applied through the use of simple skills which may be new to many who are underprivileged, often right next door or down the block.

If you are a visionary idealist, and one hopes that you share some of this sentiment, set forth on a project of developing—once you have found the target—sensible ways to help your neighbor whether he lives nearby or far away. There is some gold in some of those neglected hills of society and there is much satisfaction for contributor and recipient alike. Given in helpful and self-respecting understanding, hope and help serve both parties abundantly.

You will find in the responses you receive almost enough of the satisfactions we have been examining. You will be welcomed with open arms by all but the most inept. One must face the fact that there might be some who can't or won't respond in your same good spirit. You can be invited to visit,

REHEARSE BEFORE YOU RETIRE

contribute, to bring specific help—or to get involved in a variety of ways. You alone can make the choice and you should keep such options in your control. How much and how far do you wish to go in such do-good directions?

Write to listed agencies in the fascinating and useful yellow page sections of the telephone books of most any city. You'll find them at local telephone offices or in local libraries. Contact associations and industry groups or companies themselves. Seek out the best way in which your skills can be put to work, for gain or for satisfaction. For satisfaction—on a basis more limited than has been your full time pleasure in the past. Go to different areas and examine different opportunities. Stake out your own happy hunting ground. Test and try without fanfare the things you would like to do, projects you would like to start. What businesses would you like to try your hand at? What jobs might you wish to sample now that the big heat is off?

The basic enjoyment insurance you need is to hear again and again that there exists, and will continue to exist, a shortage of the kind of people you probably represent. People who are able and willing to bring a useful service to an existing business—or to some pressing purpose. The larger the world grows, the more complex it becomes—the more it grows service-oriented and the greater the demand for willing, able and common-sensible helpfulness. Your help and talent will be appreciated and found marketable.

Part time or full time. Any time and anywhere. You are needed somewhere and about the only question remaining is how to get across this willingness bridge—from where you are to where you want to be.

Strive to avoid too much resistance to idealism. Don't feel awkward, proud or presumptuous. Enjoy a little do-goodism in this promising and heavenly time of your life.

You have done your life's work duties. You have paid the price and earned your reward. We are told there is no reward which carries so much poetic justice, so much needed reality than that which begins the process of returning something to mankind. Help to improve the lot of those who have little—so little of the abundant gifts and so little of the concern which each of us has taken in great measure from those who have lived around us. From those who have gone before us. Typically, retirement is not the time when one wants to start over—to make a brand new pile for posterity. How typical are you?

It is measurably safer and surer to expect to enjoy your retirement if you rehearse for what you hope to retire *to*. If you take careful inventory of your personal resources. If you set your own timetable. If you establish sensible expectations. Then you have the right—and the need to promise yourself that—this I really expect to enjoy.

REHEARSE BEFORE YOU RETIRE

Go out there then and begin to enjoy your own promised land of the good retirement rewards which follow pleasant preparations.

Most retirees are amazed at how much their appreciation can be enhanced by a casual and comfortable indifference to whether it's going to be either a good or a great retirement life. Enjoy it in good health and may your years be long enough to help you pack in all the plans you will have put together.

One final hope is earnestly expressed for all of you who have come this way. May you still have so much left undone—so much you still want to do—that you wish you could ask for another lifetime in which to finish all that needs and wants to be done.

Finally—permit yourselves a freedom from concern. Welcome the joy of each extra and happy day. Worry not about tomorrow today. No looking backward at all of those yesterdays. Live today. Live a little of the loafing you have often yearned for on your life's busy days.

Remember—it's *your retirement*. So, quit! And enjoy!

ACTION IDEAS TO THINK ABOUT:
Where in the world, or where in your own familiar world—would you now wish to be?
Retirement delivers many freedoms; one of which is the chance to be almost anywhere.
Some should stay—and some enjoy trying new things in

206 REHEARSE BEFORE YOU RETIRE

new places. Use this segmented map of the USA only as a visual reminder of places available to you.

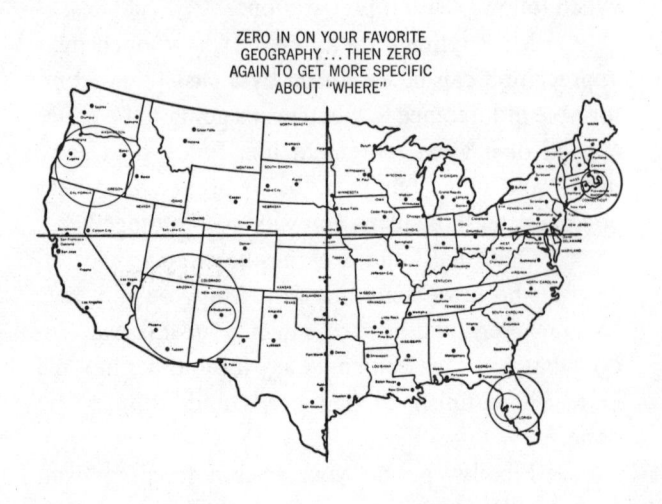

ZERO IN ON YOUR FAVORITE
GEOGRAPHY... THEN ZERO
AGAIN TO GET MORE SPECIFIC
ABOUT "WHERE"

Where to: East _____   West _____
              North _____   South _____
              Or, in between _____
              To stay _____ To move _____

REHEARSE BEFORE YOU RETIRE

NOTES ON ADDED SOURCES: *BOOKS*

Chapter 1. "BEGIN BY REHEARSING FOR YOUR RETIREMENT"

Barfield, Richard. *Early Retirement: Decisions and the Experience.* Ann Arbor: University of Michigan, 1969.

Breen, Leonard Z. and Marcus, Phillip M. *Pre-retirement Education Among Labor Unions in the United States.* Lafayette: Department of Sociology, Purdue University, 1960.

David, William. *Not Quite Ready to Retire.* Macmillan, 1970.

Otte, Elmer. *Retirement Rehearsal Guidebook.* Retirement Research, 1976. Appleton, Wisconsin.

Chapter 2. "PREPARE TO RETIRE TO SOMETHING"

Arthur, J. K. *Retire to Action.* New York: Abingdon, 1969.

Harter, Walter. *Making Money in Retirement Years.* Bantam, 1971

Zimmermann, Gereon. *The Secrets of Successful Retirement.* New York: Simon and Schuster.

Chapter 3. "ESTABLISH SENSIBLE RETIREMENT EXPECTATIONS"

Collins, Thomas. *Complete Guide to Retirement.* Prentice Hall, 1970.

Hunter, Woodrow. *Preparation for Retirement.* University of Michigan, 1968.

Chapter 4. "INVENTORY YOUR RETIREMENT RESOURCES"

Margolius, Sidney. *Personal Guide to Successful Retirement.* Random House, 1969.

Otte, Elmer. *Retirement Rehearsal Guidebook.* Retirement Research, 1976. Appleton, Wisconsin.

Laas, W. *Managing Your Money.* Popular Library, 1970.

Ford, Norman. *How to Have Money to Retire on.* New York: Harian Publications.

Lasser, Jacob. *Investing for Your Future.* Simon and Schuster, 1968.

Retirement Council. *Retirement Money Guidebook.* Harper and Row, 1963.

AARP/NRTA. *Tax Facts; A Comparative Guide.* American Association of Retired Persons, 1972. Washington, D.C.

Chapter 5. "SET YOUR OWN RETIREMENT TIMETABLE"

Mulac, Margaret E. *Leisure: Time for Living and Retirement.* 1961. Harper, New York.

Otte, Elmer. *Retirement Rehearsal Guidebook.* Retirement Research, 1976. Appleton, Wisconsin.

Hepner, H. W. *Retirement—A Time to Live Anew.* New York: McGraw Hill, 1970

Chapter 6. "Expect to Enjoy Your Retirement"

Havinghurst, R.J. *Adjustment to Retirement: A Cross-National Study.* New York: Humanities Press, 1969.

Hersey, Jean. *These Rich Years: A Journal of Retirement.* New York: Scribner, 1969.

Weisser, Edna. *On Growing Old.* New York: Houghton Mifflin, 1967.

ORGANIZATIONS:

American Association for Retired Persons, 1909 K St., N.W. Washington, D.C. 20049

Advisory Committee on Aging, Department of Health, Education and Welfare, Washington, D.C.

AFL-CIO Community Service Activities, 815 16th Street, Wash. D.C.

Council of State Chambers of Commerce, 1028 Connecticut Ave., Room 1018, Washington, D.C. 20036.

Action for Independent Maturity, Division of American Association for Retired Persons, 1909 K St., N.W. Washington, D.C. 20049 (Pre-Retirement Planning)

Order Your Own Personal Guidebook

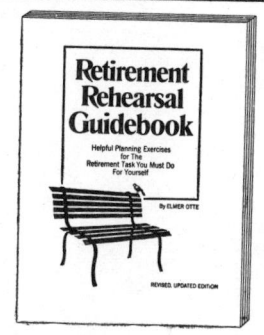

This very popular workbook is the most functional self-help planning guide available. *Retirement Rehearsal Guidebook* shows you how to chart your retirement income needs and expectations; tells how to pick your best retirement interests and activities; how to find new money opportunities in retirement; how to cope with the problems and costs of growing older, and how to make the most of the opportunities these bonus years offer you.

This *Guidebook* will become one of your family's most important record sources, a valuable heirloom.

| Single copies: **$4.95** (add 75¢ to ship) (Quantity quotes by return mail.) | Order from: **RETIREMENT RESEARCH** P.O. Box 401 Appleton, WI 54911 |